LEADERSHIP
and the
Power of Trust

Creating a High-Trust, Peak-Performance Organization

Mike Armour, Ph.D.

LIFEThemes Press
Dallas, Texas

Leadership and the Power of Trust

Printed and Bound in the
United States of America

ISBN-13: 978-0-9799398-1-5
ISBN-10: 0-9799398-1-X

Trust-Centered Leadership™ and Trust-Bonded Organization™ are registered trademarks of MCA Professional Services Group, LLC.

For additional insights: www.trustispower.com

Published by LIFEThemes Press

12700 Preston Road, Suite 285
Dallas, Texas 75230

Mailing Address:
PO Box 595609, Dallas, Texas 75359

www.LifeThemesPress.com

About the Author

As an executive coach, strategic consultant, and keynote speaker Dr. Mike Armour has served some of America's largest and best-known companies, including American Standard Trane, Bank of America, Bell Helicopter, Burlington Northern Santa Fe Railway, Comerica Bank, FritoLay, Honda, Nortel, Raytheon, TXU, and UBS Wealth Management.

Mike is the principal in Strategic Leadership Development International, based in Dallas, Texas. He also serves as the CEO of an international non-profit that operates in a dozen nations of Eastern Europe.

A life-long leader, Mike has served as the founder of a highly-successful private school, a university dean, a college president, a Navy captain, a Congressional candidate, and a key executive in a variety of non-profit and faith-based organizations. During his naval career, which spanned 35 years of active duty and reserve service, he was decorated three times for his pioneering work in computerizing the naval intelligence community.

Mike holds degrees from five colleges and universities, including a Ph.D. from UCLA. He currently works with educational and political leaders in Russia and Ukraine to create programs in ethics and character for their schools and universities.

Contents

Foreword:
The New Power Center

A new center of strategic power is quietly rising above the competitive landscape. It's the power of trust – the competitive clout of High-Trust, Peak-Performance Organizations.

To say that trust has power is no startling revelation. Trust has always held societies and organizations together. But an added dynamic is at work today. The pace of competition is now so fierce that long-term, superlative performance is absolutely vital. And sustained peak performance is possible only in settings where trust runs deep.

Unfortunately, trust is in short supply, as recent studies and surveys routinely show. Independent researchers consistently confirm a pattern of deep-seated, wholesale distrust toward leadership, corporations, and institutions, not to mention a broad distrust of government.

This trust deficit creates remarkable competitive opportunities for corporations and institutions which practice Trust-Centered Leadership™. In the post-Enron era, with leadership credibility at historic lows, people long for leaders and companies who inspire genuine trust. And because of this longing, today's trusted leaders and trusted organizations have unprecedented potential for influence and power.

And we are not speaking merely of personal influence and power. We are talking about genuine, measurable economic power. Companies with high-trust cultures are markedly more profitable than those who let trust fall into disrepair – especially over the long haul. For financial institutions, of course, trust has always been a cornerstone of success. But today trust is no less critical for industries and institutions of every stripe.

What gives trust such bottom-line leverage? The answer lies in the concept of a "learning organization," popularized in the 1990s in Peter Senge's book *The Fifth Discipline*.[1] With the information revolution in full force, the book addressed a marketplace enthralled with information as a competitive tool.

But people generally perceived this competitive power in a tactical sense. That is, the competitor with rapid access to information was in a stronger position in head-to-head, day-to-day competition.

Senge cast information and competition in a different light. He viewed information strategically, through a transformational lens. He urged companies to deploy extensive information feedback systems, then use these systems as learning tools to transform themselves.

The faster a company learns, he held, the more quickly it can implement change and remain perpetually competitive. Hence the term "learning organization." Senge quoted Arie de Geus as saying, "The ability to learn faster than your competitors may be the only sustainable competitive advantage."[2]

Experience shows that learning organizations do indeed hold superior competitive positions, perhaps more so today than when Senge first wrote. And while the competitive power of information itself may have waned, information feedback within a learning organization still conveys profound competitive strength.

Which brings us back to the subject of trust and profitability. When you look closely at today's competitive companies, they have

------

[1] Peter Senge, *The Fifth Discipline: The Art and Practice of the Learning Organization* (New York: Doubleday, 1990).
[2] Senge, *The Fifth Discipline*, p. 4.

many traits in common with a learning organization. In particular, they make constant mid-course corrections based on communication that is open, quick, and multilateral. Anything less blunts their competitive edge.

Yet this kind of communication, coupled with an on-going process of transformation, demands high levels of trust. Trust eliminates corporate barriers that otherwise choke off arteries of communication, thwart rapid change, and impede innovation.

The higher the trust, the more readily a company can learn, re-evaluate, and change. If the speed at which we learn is our "only sustainable competitive advantage," to quote Arie de Geuss once more, then the key to that advantage is a high-trust culture that empowers an organization to learn quickly. That's why, with trust in short supply, today's new center of power is trust.

Note: For more insights on themes developed in this book, visit www.trustispower.com.

The High Cost of Low Trust

Tested Under Fire

L
ost in a fog of unanswered questions, I eased into the parking spot marked "President," turned off the engine, and took a deep breath. Today, at age 37, I was plunging into the most daunting leadership challenge of my life.

Gazing across the campus, now deserted for summer vacation, I wondered whether it would look much different in September. After 15 months without a president, the college was in trouble. Deep trouble. And everyone knew it.

Over the previous two years enrollment had plummeted by a third. And forecasts for the fall promised more of the same.

Financially we were in a tailspin, as well. Every day brought new crises. Salaries were months in arrears. And the school was 90 days overdue on one-fifth of its payables for the year.

To say the least, the road ahead was steep and difficult. So why should anyone go with me? Why should students return? Why should faculty remain? Why should donors recommit?

And most of all, what would it require of me as a leader for us to survive?

Turnarounds are never easy, whatever your business. But they are particularly difficult for colleges and universities.

For one thing, success hinges on a single "sales day" each year. That "sales day" is fall registration. If "sales" are weak at fall registration, cash flow suffers for the next twelve months. There's no option for a mid-term sales promotion to draw in more customers and generate cash. And since enrollment usually drops in the spring, cashflow constraints grow more excruciating as the year unfolds.

Moreover, a bad sales day at the freshman level is doubly disastrous. It dooms the school to four or five years of financial anguish. As attrition takes its toll, the small freshman class turns into a tiny senior class, which imposes a crushing cost-per-student ratio on upper division courses.

Shortly after I arrived on campus we experienced our third consecutive year of bad sales days. And this one was our worst by far. I quickly discovered that there were no "how to" books for turning around a situation like this. I was flying entirely by the seat of my pants, responding as much from instinct as know-how.

These instincts told me that nothing was more urgent than building as much internal trust on campus as possible. We needed deep, deep trust – trust so strong that it would hold us together, whatever came our way.

At the time I had no name for the principles I was putting into practice. (It was two decades later before I began referring to them collectively as Trust-Centered Leadership™.) But I believed without reservation in the power of trust. And I was convinced that trust-building was paramount for anyone in my position of leadership.

As we persevered in the turnaround, Trust-Centered Leadership™ grew from a loose set of instincts to a purposeful management approach. Four years later, when I resigned in exhaustion, we were still not fully recovered. But enrollment had rebounded. Most bills were current. And we were looking ahead to a major capital campaign. The school at least had a new lease on life.

Remarkably, over this entire period we lost only five or six employees due to payroll uncertainties. And we set several new milestones in donor and foundation support. I will always wish we could have done more. But without the trust we built, we would have achieved far less.

For me, therefore, Trust-Centered Leadership™ is not some ethereal theory. It's something that I have tested under fire, in the most withering of circumstances. I know firsthand that it works.

Jack Be Nimble . . . Or Else

I have an early childhood memory of standing at a bedroom window, staring across the yard and reciting nursery rhymes. One of my favorites was

Jack, be nimble. Jack, be quick.
Jack, jump over the candlestick.

(My lisping version, however, had him jumping over a "candle thtick.")

Now, decades later, I'm talking once more about Jack and the candlestick, this time to corporate leaders and executives. The obstacles they face are obviously more challenging than mere candlesticks.

But to get over these hurdles, they need an organization that is just like Jack, quick and nimble. To quote Xerox CEO Anne Mulcahy, "If you're not nimble, there's no advantage to size. It's like a rock."[3]

The reason is simple. Today's business world is no longer merely competitive. It's hypercompetitive. As *Fortune* magazine recently put it, "We're competing with more people in more places in more ways than ever before."[4] Your industry, like every industry, feels the incessant pressure of fierce and now global competition.

---

[3] Quoted in Betsy Morris, "The New Rules," *Fortune* (July 24, 2006), pp. 70-87.

[4] Rick Kirkland, "Will the U.S. Be Flattened by a Flatter World?", *Fortune* (June 7, 2005), pp. 47-48.

To succeed, if not survive, three things are essential:

- agility
- speed and
- innovation

The agility to turn on a dime. The speed to be fast on your feet. The innovation to stay ahead of the pack.

These three – agility, speed, and innovation – are king-makers in today's business world. Failure to pay them homage can prove deadly. With markets, industries, and technology changing at a staggering pace, we must either adapt quickly or risk being swept aside.

One-room schools of our frontier past taught the so-called "three R's" of reading, writing, and arithmetic. Now, living on the new frontier of a global economy, we must master another set of three R's.

- *The first is Rapid Response.* Customers are unapologetic about their demands. They want swift service, prompt delivery, and instant access to information. And empowered by the internet, they are quite discriminating in where they buy and what they pay. If you don't cater to their whims, they seek out someone who does. Even someone continents away.

- *The second R is Rapid Recalibration.* Market forces and competitive environments are in constant flux. Today's dynamite idea quickly becomes tomorrow's disaster. And this principle holds true whether we are talking about products, services, organizational design, production techniques, logistics systems, or marketing campaigns. In order to thrive, companies must make constant mid-course corrections based on accurate feedback from open, unhampered, and multi-lateral communication.

- *The third is R is Rapid Realignment*. Sometimes mere recalibration is not enough. Complete transformation is necessary. And when such moments come, companies must be
  able to repackage themselves quickly, almost instinctively,
  in the face of new realities. Otherwise they are likely to be
  left in the dust by more innovative peers.

In effect, the "Three R's" are returning us to the sage advice of
the nursery rhyme: Jack, be nimble; Jack, be quick. Agility, speed,
innovation.

Agility, speed, and innovation are king-makers in today's business world. Failure to pay them homage can prove deadly.

It's hardly a new message, of course. We've designed organizations for decades to be faster, more flexible, more adept at change.
But the pace is becoming relentless.

Development cycles are now compressed to the extreme. Lead
times have evaporated. Customer expectations stand at all-time
highs, customer patience at all-time lows.

Under the weight of this unyielding pressure, leaders are
squeezing every possible ounce of performance from their companies. Even incremental enhancements, they know, hold the promise
of competitive leverage.

From this perspective, contemporary managers are much like
NASCAR pit crews, endlessly fine-tuning performance. Pit crews
are the epitome of Jack's quick and nimble style. Their first objective is to engineer a machine that is itself quick and nimble. Their
second objective, equally critical, is to build a team that is just as
quick and nimble as their machine.

To this end, nothing is left to chance. Pit stops are carefully or-
chestrated, every move artfully choreographed, to eliminate even a
single wasted motion. Races are lost in split second delays.

Management, too, has a "machine" to keep in peak performance, with tools that go by names like right-sizing, outsourcing, systems integration, and just-in-time delivery. And like a pit crew, successful leaders and managers are passionate about maximizing their own personal performance as a team.

Wasted time, whether in decision-making or implementation, means lost momentum, missed opportunities, and sacrificed profits. And it can cost the race, as well.

Picking up on this theme, *Business Week* blazoned a pivotal question across the cover of its March 27, 2006 issue, asking in huge block letters, "Is your company fast enough?" The cover article zeroed in on innovations that have cut time-to-market in half since the turn of the millennium, reducing development cycles by months and even years.[5]

The article concludes by quoting Bruce Richardson of AMR Research Inc., who tersely observes, "There are two kinds of businesses: the quick and the dead." Richardson, too, apparently subscribes to the "Jack-be-nimble" philosophy of leadership.

While the authors acknowledge that Richardson may have overstated the urgency of being quick, they nonetheless concede, "In an era when once-mighty dinosaurs are struggling to survive, the alternative to fast and lean may soon be . . . gone."

---

[5] Steve Hamm, "Speed Demons: How Smart Companies are Creating New Products – and Whole New Businesses – Almost Overnight," *Business Week* (March 27, 2006), pp. 69-76.

3

The Performance Catalyst

I'm frequently asked to help organizations become more "quick and nimble" by dealing with issues that mire down speed and momentum.

Clients usually come to me with a general idea of where the trouble lies. "We have a problem with communication," they say. Or morale. Or dedication. Or customer service.

But as I peel back these problems, layer by layer, I discover a common culprit lurking underneath. It's best described as a network of debilitating trust issues that have gone unrecognized, unaddressed, or unresolved.

These issues are often so far from sight, or else so cleverly disguised, that management has not sensed their presence, much less their magnitude.

Yet this kind of "silent distrust" invariably takes its toll on speed and momentum. This toll may not be readily apparent. But it's always there. By its very nature distrust gums up the works. Thwarts change. Bogs things down. Protects turf. And chokes off open communication.

In a word, distrust takes away the very attributes that make for a quick and nimble organization. Distrust nails Jacks feet to the floor so that he can no longer jump over the candlestick.

Trust, on the other hand, is a performance catalyst. A performance turbo-charger. It puts spring in Jack's feet. To see this inherent leverage, simply ask yourself questions like this.

- How swiftly can an organization reconfigure itself, transform itself, or reposition itself in the marketplace?
- How quickly can it innovate? Diversify? Bring new products on line?

The answer always depends on trust. To the degree that distrust prevails, time and speed are lost.

For this reason, we cannot optimize competitive advantage – certainly not *sustainable* advantage – unless we first optimize trust. Our leadership objective must go beyond simply building a high-performance organization. We must instead set our sights on nothing less than a High-Trust, Peak-Performance Organization.

We cannot optimize sustainable competitive advantage unless we first optimize trust.

In their book *Built on Trust*, Arky Ciancutti and Thomas Steding lay out an artful description of how trust creates competitive advantage:

> In an atmosphere of trust and support, different points of view can be expressed openly and safely. People feel free to speak their minds and contribute their unique wisdom without fear of recrimination or ridicule. This gives the team access to more information and more energy. Leadership organizations harvest the exponential intelligence that diversity affords them, and use it to create their competitive advantage.[6]

trust is a force multiplier

To borrow a military term, trust is a force multiplier. Force multipliers are technologies and techniques that give military units

---

[6] Arky Ciancutti and Thomas L. Steding, *Built on Trust: Gaining Competitive Advantage in Any Organization* (Chicago: Contemporary Books, 2000), p. 16.

strength, power, and ability far beyond what seems feasible for units of such size. And that's precisely what trust does in any human enterprise. Speed, agility, and innovation bestow competitive advantage. But they reach their full potential only in settings of high trust.

High thrust performance in the marketplace starts with high-trust relationships in your organization.

In high-trust cultures things run more smoothly. More quickly. More profitably.

- Marketing is more cost-effective, because it's easier to retain preferred customers.

- Turnover drops sharply, because talented workers are eager to stay.

- Feedback is quicker, because there's no fear of retaliation.

- Learning is faster, because it's safe to admit what you don't know.

- Communication is more transparent. Morale is higher. Productivity is greater. Commitment is deeper.

Harvard Business Review recently held that executives make better and more creative decisions in high-trust settings.[7]

In a word, trust is power. Competitive power. High thrust performance in the marketplace starts with high-trust relationships in your organization.

---

[7] Edward M. Hallowell, "Overloaded Circuits: Why Smart People Underperform," *Harvard Business Review* (January 2005), pp. 55-62.

trust makes $

4

The Economics of Trust

Trust has measurable financial impact, reflected on the bottom line. That's the conclusion from a study of 7500 workers by Watson Wyatt Worldwide Consulting.

Their research (conducted in 2000) documented the positive correlation between high levels of employee trust and the payback to shareholders. In companies where trust was high, shareholder returns were 43% higher than in low-trust companies.[8]

Equally striking are findings at the QVC Home Shopping Network. QVC surveys their customers extensively, asking respondents to rate the company in terms of trustworthiness. A seven-point scale is used, with seven being the highest.

Most companies would be pleased with consistent ratings of six. But QVC has learned that people who rate the company at seven are 80% more likely to make repeat purchases than those who give it a score of six.[9]

Similarly, research at Case Western Reserve University shows the decisive power of trust when it's time to buy. The study asked people to identify the most critical factors in their decisions to make a purchase.

---

[8] Bruce N. Pfau, "Employee Satisfaction Proves Crucial to Shareholder Value," *Strategy@Work*, found October 25, 2005 at http://www.watsonwyatt.com/strategyatwork/articles/2000/2000_04_ai.asp.
[9] John Hunter, "I Want My QVC," *CIO Magazine* (July 14, 2003), found April 19, 2007 at http://cio.com.au/index.php/id;127536714;fp;4;fpid;1;pf;1.

`For consumers the two most decisive factors were trust and perceived value, with perceived value ranked first by only a slim margin. In business-to-business transactions, however, the same researchers discovered that trust outranks perceived value. Companies are willing to pay more, it seems, to do business with those they trust.[10]

"If you don't have trust inside your company, then you can't transfer it to your customers."

– Roger Staubach

Customer trust, in turn, depends on levels of trust within your organization. In the words of Roger Staubach, the legendary Dallas business leader and Hall of Fame quarterback, "If you don't have trust inside your company, then you can't transfer it to your customers."[11] And research tends to bear him out.

Fortune magazine annually publishes a list of the hundred best companies to work for in America. The Great Place to Work Institute, which compiles the list, has studied the American workplace for over 20 years. They have reached the conclusion that "trust between managers and employees is THE primary defining characteristic of the very best workplaces."[12]

When I cite these kinds of statements and statistics, I get occasional pushback worded like this: "Company X is making a ton of money, and I know for a fact that there is deep, deep distrust in their organization."

Recently, in fact, a highly successful attorney made this very observation to me about his own firm. "Everyone knows there's a lot of distrust among principals in our company," he said, "but we have

---

[10] Jeff Beudix, "Can You Trust Customer Trust?", found October 24, 2005 at http://www.case.edu/pubs/cnews/2000/12-14/singh.htm.

[11] Jerry Kavanaugh, "Q&A: Roger Staubach," *Dallas Business Journal* (January 14, 2005).

[12] Great Places to Work Institute Home Page, found June 10, 2006 at http://www.greatplacestowork.com.

never made so much money in our history. It's hard to build the case that distrust is costing us money."

I immediately replied, "And what is your turnover rate? How much of your budget each year goes to replacing key players who walk out the door?" He quickly acknowledged that the defection rate was sobering

"And does the distrust have anything to do with their departure?" I continued. He reflected momentarily, then answered with a nod.

I then inquired, "How much does it cost to replace each person who leaves?" He quoted a number that was fairly close to the national average for major law firms, which is about $300,000 to replace a solid performer.

"So if we multiply that cost by the number of people who are leaving each year," I went on, "then add in the volume of business that follows them out the door, that's how much money you are leaving on the table because of distrust."

Low trust and high turnover love to work shoulder to shoulder.

The reason I moved so quickly to their turnover rate is that low trust and high turnover love to work shoulder to shoulder. When companies are struggling to stay competitive and financially sound, it's easy to show how distrust and excessive turnover are putting them at a competitive disadvantage.

But in settings that are highly profitable, like my friend's law firm, management can blithely ignore distrust, assuming that its impact is inconsequential. After all, cash is flowing in torrents. Only against the backdrop of high turnover costs do we begin to see how just much distrust is draining the bottom line.

Due to shifting demographics, the challenge of limiting turnover costs will grow exponentially in the foreseeable future. With the baby boomers hitting retirement years, a rapidly graying workforce is already giving way to a much younger one.[13] This transition, in and of itself, adds immense turnover costs. But the greater turnover challenge lies elsewhere.

We are quickly learning that today's youngest workers are a breed apart from co-workers twenty or thirty years their senior. Compared to previous generations, the twenty-and-thirty-somethings in our organizations are less willing to sacrifice family life and personal fulfillment to advance their careers.

A high-trust culture reduces the opportunity for dissatisfaction and disillusionment.

They have also entered the workforce assuming frequent job changes over the course of their professional life. Given this expectation, they readily pack up and leave when they become dissatisfied or disillusioned or when work demands impinge on life-balance commitments. Long-term loyalty is a scarce commodity.

A high-trust culture, by its very nature, reduces the opportunity for dissatisfaction and disillusionment. A high-trust culture yields an atmosphere that tends to be healthy, positive, and energizing, the very kind of workplace that younger men and women demand.

Noting this fact, a vice-president for a Fortune 200 company lamented to me, "Our company does not yet realize how vital trust is for holding workers. Because we are one of those rare companies that still offers exceptional pension plans, older workers are sticking around to claim their retirement. They put up with outmoded management styles that won't be tolerated by the younger workers who will replace them. I'm afraid that we are about to be hit squarely in the face with that reality."

---

[13] Of the workers between 25 and 54, six in ten are baby-boomers, and in some fields (such as science and technology) more than half the workers are over 40. Richard Florida, "America's Looming Creativity Crisis," *Harvard Business Review* (May 2004), p. 58.

As the workforce "youthens" (to borrow a term from King Arthur in *Camelot*), high-trust cultures will be one of the most important resources for holding turnover costs in line. In these cultures leadership will abandon the final vestiges of those outmoded management styles that impair trust, becoming instead purposeful about trust-building. Otherwise, they will leave themselves at a financial and competitive disadvantage as turnover exacts a needless toll on the bottom line.

high trust reduces turnover!

few companies have a plan to build trust

5

Strategic Trust

T he deeper trust runs in your organization, the greater the potential for stellar achievement. That fact alone makes trust-building a strategic priority.

Yet, while I frequently see trust catalogued in corporate values, I know few companies with a strategic plan for building trust. Perhaps there was once a time when we could safely treat trust-building as something less than a strategic issue. But no longer.

Global competition has become too fierce, margins too thin, product cycles too compressed – and most of all, the stakes have become too high – for us to settle for anything less than a Trust-Bonded Organization™.

Change itself is undercutting the very trust we need to survive its impact.

The tireless pace of change is putting unprecedented strain on companies everywhere. Whether they break under the strain or grow stronger is largely a function of how much employees trust their leadership, their fellow-workers, the overall organization, and its products and services.

Unfortunately, change itself is undercutting the very trust we need to survive its impact. The mere talk of change, much less its implementation, touches off uncertainty, anxiety, and fear – always fertile soil for distrust. And as change accelerates, trust is apparently reaching new lows in the American workplace, as we shall see later.

Thus, if it's naïve to ignore change as a strategic issue, it's certainly naïve to treat trust-building as a peripheral concern. For today's leaders, trust-building must be a core discipline, both within their organizations and in their personal leadership style.

As its name implies, Trust-Centered Leadership™ puts trust-building at the heart of the strategic agenda. Trust-Centered Leadership™ weighs every decision, every action, and every initiative against the goal of maximizing trust:

- First, maximizing the trust the organization has in its leaders.
- Then maximizing a culture of trust across the entire organization.
- And third, maximizing the trust of both internal and external customers.

To achieve these goals, Trust-Centered Leadership™ pursues "trust-friendliness" in four critical arenas, which we might label Climate, Character, Conduct, and Culture. *4*

1. A Climate Conducive to Trust. For trust to prosper, the right atmosphere is required. Responsibility for creating this atmosphere devolves on us as leaders, for leadership always has the critical task of setting the organization's tone. Leaders must actively promote specific qualities in their organizational climate if trust is to find a receptive atmosphere. We examine these qualities later, when we introduce the SIRVU formula.

2. Character. Trust does not endure in the absence of trustworthy character. No one can build a Trust-Bonded Organization™ without principled players and trustworthy leaders. Through our example as leaders we set the mark for character in our organization. After all, we cannot expect people to live up to standards which we do not model ourselves. For people to grant us unqualified trust, they must see exemplary character in us. Then, and only then, will we have the credibility to challenge broader issues of character within the group.

3. Conduct. In a business context, conduct is the single greatest determinant of trust. Conduct is the medium through which climate, character, and culture reveal themselves. At the same time, conduct also feeds back into corporate climate and culture to recolor and remold them. As a leader your primary mechanisms for establishing a climate and culture of trust are the standards of conduct that you mandate, model, sanction, encourage, and enforce.

4. A Culture that Is Purposeful About Building Trust. "Trust-friendliness," even if it permeates climate, character, and conduct, is no assurance that a culture of trust actually exists, certainly not one strong enough to weather the demands of today's relentless competitive pace. A culture of trust (to trace the word "culture" back to its Latin roots) must be purposively and intentionally "cultivated," not just left to emerge on its own. For Trust-Centered Leadership™, creating a culture of trust is a strategic objective second to none.

––––––––––––––––––––

There have always been leaders, of course, who, while quite effective, evidenced little concern with trust-building. We would never suggest, therefore, that Trust-Centered Leadership™ is the only appropriate paradigm from which to lead. (In fact, I have published on other leadership paradigms, which I frequently teach.)

But if our goal is to build competitive strength in a hypercompetitive marketplace and to maximize the clout of the three kingmakers – agility, speed, and innovation – we have no choice but to optimize trust.

6

A Harvest of Weeds

G rowing up on a farm, I soon learned that crops flourish only in fertile soil which is carefully tended. Weeds, on the other hand, thrive almost anywhere. And you don't have to plant them. They just show up.

In the same way, trust must be cultivated and cared for. Distrust, on the other hand, seems to spawn effortlessly, almost spontaneously, and spreads rapidly on its own.

When my brother was about 12, he persuaded Mom to let him plant a garden that covered a fourth of the backyard. He worked tirelessly at the task through the spring, tilling the soil, laying out his rows, fertilizing the seedlings. Soon his crops stood healthy and strong.

Then he left for summer camp, where he met a new friend who invited him to Canada for two weeks. So off he went. On his return he hurriedly greeted the family, then bounded out the backdoor to visit his garden. Who could ever forget his crest-fallen face when he saw his prize plants now overgrown and choked with weeds!

Distrust, like those weeds, requires no encouragement in order to spread. All it needs is a leadership that takes trust for granted, a leadership that quits tending the soil and ignores the task of actively nurturing trust.

Every action a leader takes either purposefully cultivates trust, or it creates an opening for seeds of distrust to take root. Knowing how quickly distrust can spread, Trust-Centered Leadership™

keeps the proactive task of trust-building at the top of its daily agenda.

Trust-Centered Leadership™ does not replace other styles of leadership, like some flavor of the month. Rather, it comes alongside them, giving them added leverage. Added power. Added impact. It turbo-charges performance. When coupled with principles of Trust-Centered Leadership™, every responsible leadership philosophy gains enhanced effectiveness.

Every action a leader takes either purposefully cultivates trust, or it creates an opening for seeds of distrust to take root.

Trust-Centered Leadership™ is not merely for organizations with glaring trust problems. It's also for organizations who already have a strong culture of trust, but who know that trust is forever vulnerable. In healthy organizations Trust-Centered Leadership™ maintains competitive momentum by denying distrust the soil in which to propagate.

If weeds infest your lawn, you have two options for attacking the problem. One choice is to go after the invaders with weed killer. It's a quick solution, but it threatens toxic side effects. And usually, after only a few weeks, the weeds pop up again.

The other approach is to create such a healthy lawn that weeds cannot flourish. This approach is longer-lasting, systemic, and proactive.

Trust-Centered Leadership™ takes the second approach. Not that Trust-Centered Leadership™ never breaks out the weed killer. Sometimes conditions demand it. But Trust-Centered Leadership™ is primarily about longer-term, more enduring solutions to the trust challenge.

The primary way to create a weed-free lawn is not by playing defense, mounting an attack on every weed that appears. Rather, the best strategy is to play offense, creating such vibrant turf that weeds can't make a stand. We fight distrust the same way we fight weeds, by actively promoting health.

Some have said that to interest companies and corporations in Trust-Centered Leadership™ we must focus on the economic advantages of trust, not the health-building benefits. I argue that you cannot separate the two. What makes high-trust companies profitable is that workers are exceptionally motivated and engaged as a result of their enthusiasm for a healthy workplace setting.

To succeed, trust-building must be as much about fostering a healthy work environment as it is about enhancing profits and competitive advantage.

Should leadership decide to focus on trust solely to improve profitability – even if leaders disguise the initiative in language of "creating a better workplace" – workers are shrewd enough to see through the ploy. They will soon recognize that management's true fervor is for profits, not workplace quality.

Once that recognition sets in, the program to expand trust actually yields the opposite effect and works to undermine trust. In the eyes of employees, trust-building has been reduced to a mere tactic. It is no longer seen as vital to the core ethos of the organization. And that's a deadly perception.

To succeed, trust-building must be as much about fostering a healthy work environment as it is about enhancing profits and competitive advantage. Trust-Centered Leadership™ aims at building the kind of healthy workplace that is implied by the phrase "high-trust culture," confident that this approach pays a second dividend by improving the bottom line through efficiency, speed, and performance.

7

No Drag, Just Performance

I n competitive environments, riveted on peak performance, there are only two ways to increase speed. The first is to increase power. The second is to reduce drag. For NASCAR pit crews these are two entirely different undertakings. Nothing they do to increase the power of their vehicle reduces drag as well.

Leadership, on the other hand, can boost power and diminish drag simultaneously merely by enlarging trust. High levels of trust accelerate open communication, collaboration, and feedback, while giving people confidence to take the initiative and make timely decisions.

These traits are imperative, of course, if we are to maintain cutting-edge momentum and innovation. At the same time, by dislodging distrust, we rid the organization of a heavy foot on the brake and unleash pent-up potential.

Tim Gallwey, author of *The Inner World of Tennis* and a number of related titles, is the dean of performance coaching. Gallwey's fundamental formula is simple: potential minus interference equals performance. He puts his emphasis on removing interference, convinced that improved performance will then emerge almost naturally.

In a similar fashion, by eliminating interference created by distrust, Trust-Centered Leadership™ gives free rein to the potential within your organization.

$$potential - interference = performance$$

And should you encounter heavy seas, Trust-Centered Leadership™ pays an added dividend. In times of crisis, change, or challenge, people rally most readily around leaders whom they trust.

As a consequence, a culture of trust gives organizations the resilience to weather disruptive change, rebound from major setbacks, and transcend adversity. Indeed, when "the going gets rough," trust is the leader's most powerful ally.

When "the going gets rough," trust is the leader's most powerful ally.

Trust-Centered Leadership™ thus combines the competitive advantage of speed with the staying-power to survive even determined storms. I know this survival power first-hand from my years of leading a campus turnaround as a college president. Not a day went by without drawing on trust to hold the team together in the face of financial uncertainty, looming setbacks, and dispiriting developments.

Because trust builds both bonds and speed, I like to describe it as the glue that holds an organization together and the lubricant that allows it to run smoothly, even in times of disruptive change. Since no other substance is both glue and lubricant, I jokingly refer to trust as "glue-bricant."

Yet jokes aside, we must never make light of trust-building itself. Agility, speed, and innovation may be today's king-makers in business. But trust is the power behind the throne. Without it, King Jack could never be quick and nimble enough to succeed.

However, being momentarily quick and nimble does not necessarily mean that trust prevails, since bursts of speed and innovation are occasionally possible in the absence of high trust. But unless trust is increased, these moments cannot sustain themselves. Their success will prove short-lived, at best.

Years ago, as a young intelligence officer, I was impressed with the graceful lines and reported thrust of Soviet fighter aircraft. Then one day I had a clandestine opportunity to examine one of the latest Russian designs firsthand.

As I approached the craft, what struck me immediately was not its graceful lines, but the amount of drag it had to overcome. The plates that formed the skin of the fuselage had been joined together with weld beads as wide as my little finger.

No wonder this bird needed so much thrust! As the plane approached combat speeds, friction and drag from the weld beads must have generated immense resistance. The Russians were obviously overcoming the problem with brute force.

Brute force (most notably in the form of tremendous outlays of capital) may occasionally overcome the drag of widespread distrust and fuel an organization's brief foray into impressive innovation and speed-to-market.

The vital question, however, is whether this level of performance can be maintained long-term when trust is in short supply. What happens when there are no longer enough resources to sustain the brute force? The answer, of course, is that the drag of distrust will once more slow things to a pace that is mediocre, or perhaps worse.

Many organizations know the drag of distrust all too well. For them Trust-Centered Leadership™ is an essential first step in making themselves competitive. But it is not a quick fix. Building a Trust-Bonded Organization™ takes time, focus, and persistence. Maintaining trust, once built, is equally demanding.

To date, few have seemed willing to pay the price in time, energy, and focus to create a truly Trust-Bonded Organization™. The result is what I call a spiraling trust-deficit, the subject of chapter eight. Research demonstrates that trust is at shockingly low levels within corporate America.

Thus, while trust is theoretically accessible to everyone as a competitive tool, high-trust cultures remain notably uncommon. So long as this remains the case, the very scarcity of trust will give Trust-Bonded Organizations™ a competitive edge.

We noted earlier the cover of *Business Week* which asked, "Is your company fast enough?" The accompanying article concluded that "speed-to-market is now the ultimate competitive weapon."

But let me question that conclusion. I would argue that speed-to-market, while clearly a competitive weapon, is not the *ultimate* competitive weapon. Trust deserves that title. Without trust an organization cannot be agile, quick, and innovative enough to remain a top competitor.

We have now entered a day when high-trust cultures are as vital to competitive success as is access to markets, capital, and information. Trust is power. Sustaining power. Competitive power. Strategic power. And because it is in such short supply, trust is more pivotal and more powerful than ever.

8

Our Spiraling Trust Deficit (And What It Costs Us)

Recently the Discovery Channel reconstructed the final moments of a famous flight of five Navy Avengers that disappeared in the Bermuda Triangle during the Second World War. Using records from radio intercepts ashore, the film recreated the dialogue among the pilots as their situation grew more desperate.

From these intercepts it's clear that the lieutenant leading the formation was disoriented. He complained to ground stations that his compass was apparently not working. Against the advice of other flight members, who still had faith in their compass readings, he took a heading that actually doomed the flight.

The mounting distrust of the other pilots is evident in their transmissions. But they never broke formation, never violated their military discipline. Instead, they choked back their distrust and continued to follow, eventually running out of fuel and plunging to their death in the open Atlantic.

Toward the end it was evident that the pilots were no longer remaining in formation because they believed in their leader. Instead, they were hoping to help one another in the water once the inevitable ditching occurred. It was thus their loyalty to one another, not so much their loyalty to the leader, that held them together as the end drew near.

Outside of organizations with military-like discipline, people rarely follow a leader who has lost their trust. They may "hang around" for self-serving reasons. Perhaps to have a pay check while looking for another job. Or to hold onto their benefits. Or to see if a turnaround occurs in short order. Or like those young pilots, they may hang around out of loyalty to their buddies. But they are no longer followers. Not in the truest sense of the word. They are instead merely a presence.

Workers who simply "hang around" may actually look like genuine followers. They may show up on time. Put in a full day. Continue to fulfill basic expectations. And if their work ethic is strong enough, they might even be labeled as committed.

While no one factor accounts for workers being unengaged, distrust is a primary culprit.

But in reality they have merely acquiesced to an authority structure which no longer commands their trust or respect. As Peter Senge points out in *The Fifth Discipline*, what they evidence is not commitment, but compliance.[14] They comply with the rules. They comply with minimum standards. But they are no longer passionate about excellence, either for themselves or for their organization. They are (to use a more recent management buzz word) unengaged.

Unengaged workers are the arch-enemy of lasting competitive advantage. And if the Gallup Organization is correct, it's an enemy that is well entrenched. Based on extensive research, Gallup classifies fewer than a third of American workers as truly engaged.[15] The

---

[14] Senge, *The Fifth Discipline*, pp. 218-20.

[15] "Gallup Study Finds That Many Employees Doubt the Ethics of Corporate Leaders," *Gallup Management Journal* (October 10, 2002), found March 22, 2006 at http://gmj.gallup.com/content/829/Gallup-Study-Finds-That-Many-Employees-Doubt-the.aspx.

majority, to use Senge's description, are at best compliant. They are non-engaged.

While no one factor accounts for this wholesale non-engagement, distrust is a primary culprit.

- In a survey of 7500 workers in 2004 by Watson Wyatt Worldwide, 50% of the respondents registered distrust of senior management.[16]

- Two years earlier another Watson Wyatt poll of 13,000 workers found only 39% of them expressing trust in the senior leadership of their companies.[17]

- In July 2002 the Gallup Organization and the financial services firm UBS surveyed 600 private-sector workers, of whom only 48% said they believe corporate executives are honest and ethical.[18]

- A poll of 1792 workers by Peter Hart Research found that almost two-thirds of them do not trust their company to treat workers fairly.[19]

- This was borne out in another survey by CareerBuilders.com, in which 30% described corporate leadership as untrustworthy.[20]

---

[16] Wendy Phaneuf, "Building Team Loyalty And Commitment: Employee Loyalty Is a Matter of Trust," found July 20, 2007 at http://advisor.com/doc/18086.

[17] Steve Bates, "Employees Losing Faith in Leaders, Surveys Find," *HR Magazine* (September 2002).

[18] *Ibid.*

[19] "'Workers' Rights In America' Survey: Majority Says Management Has too much Power," August 30, 2001 found May 15, 2007 at http://archives.cnn.com/2001/CAREER/trends/08/30/afl.cio.study/index.html.

[20] "CareerBuilder Survey Finds Growing Worker Disenchantment, Long Hours and Stress," survey conducted August 2001, found July 17, 2007 at http://www.careerbuilder.com.

- A survey performed by Manchester Consulting at 325 companies in 12 industries placed the average level of trust in these companies at 5.1 on a ten-point scale.[21]

- The same survey found two out of every three executives saying that trust had diminished within their organization over the preceding two years. This led Manchester Senior Vice President Lew Stern, who has studied workplace trust for two decades, to describe trust in corporate America at an all-time low.[22]

- In another survey of 450 executives in 30 industries, only half of the managers expressed trust in their leaders.[23]

- When the Council of Public Relations Firms did a national survey of 1013 workers, two-thirds said that their management's communication is not consistently truthful and open.[24]

- A survey of 800 Americans by the University of Chicago in 2002 found roughly four out of five expressing very limited confidence in the people who run major corporations.[25]

- A study by the Conference Board, released in 2003, indicated that only 23% of Americans trust corporate executives[26].

- The study also discovered that public trust in CEOs was lower than for any profession other than used car salesmen.

---

[21] "Workplace Trust in Decline, According to Survey Finding," found May 26, 2006 at http://www.ibew1613.org/library/notrust.html.

[22] Dell Poncet, "Trust Is A Bust," *Philadelphia Business Journal*, September 12, 1997.

[23] Robert Hurley, "The Decision to Trust," *Harvard Business Review*, September 2006, p. 55.

[24] Wally Bock, "Trust in the Boss," found March 12, 2007 at http://www.mondaymemo.net/010902feature.htm.

[25] Hurley, "The Decision to Trust," p. 55.

[26] "The Blue-Ribbon Commission on Public Trust and Private Enterprise," The Conference Board, January 2003.

This was the first time in the history of the survey for corporate chief executives to rank so low.

- A study in 2005 by Mercer Human Resources Consulting indicated that only 40% of employees trust top management to communicate honestly with them.[27]

- And when the Aon Institute studied 1800 workers, it discovered that one in eight distrust their employer at the most fundamental level of keeping them safe from fear, harassment, and intimidation at work.[28]

Corporate America, in other words, is running a trust deficit. It's as glaring as our trade deficit and no less damaging to the bottom line. To the degree that companies fail to recognize a climate of distrust – or worse, choose to ignore it – they surrender competitive advantage. They start down a trail which leads

- from lost trust to lost commitment
- from lost commitment to lost engagement
- from lost engagement to lost competitive power

Perhaps the most telling indicator of endemic distrust is the diminishing number of workers who are willing to consider middle management positions. One writer recently identified three factors which seem to leave these young workers disillusioned with middle management careers.

The first is a concern with job security. Younger workers generally perceive that middle management positions are most likely to be eliminated following a merger or acquisition. They don't trust ownership to protect them if the company changes hands.

The second concern is the limited ability to maintain a proper work-life balance in today's high-demand middle management envi-

---

[27] "US Employees' Trust in Management is Low" found April 25, 2007 at http://marketinghire.com/careers/surveys/1105/trust_in_management_low.htm.

[28] Sue Shellenbarger, "Employee Trust among Most Important Assets," *The Milwaukee Journal Sentinel*, July 12, 2000.

ronment. And third is the sense that joining middle management means becoming part of a team that is viewed with distrust.[29]

The article quotes Terry Bacon, whose research we will notice later, as saying:

> A key reason there is less interest in middle management is because there is an extraordinary amount of distrust in management today. Who wants to be in a position where you're distrusted and working with a disengaged workforce? [Younger workers] don't view climbing up the ladder as success."

Corporate America is running a trust deficit as glaring as our trade deficit and no less damaging to the bottom line.

A disengaged workforce, as we have seen, is a by-product of lost trust. Thus, our current middle management crisis is being aggravated both by lost trust toward management and lost trust among workers.

Trade deficits may sometimes be helpful, or so we've been told. But trust deficits are never beneficial. They sap energy, giving nothing in return. Even worse, they thwart every effort to be quick and nimble – like Jack.

No one chronicles our trust deficit more persistently than a bland little guy named Dilbert and the comic strip that bears his name.

What accounts for his phenomenal popularity? Why do Dilbert calendars sprout everywhere on employee desks? And why are Dilbert cartoons tacked prominently on cubicle walls?

It's because Dilbert strikes a resonant chord in millions of readers. He reminds them daily of their own place of work.

---

[29] Stephanie Armour, "Who Wants To Be a Middle Manager?", *USA Today* (August 13, 2007), Section B, pp. 1-2.

And how would we describe Dilbert's workplace? It's a world of cynicism. Of turf-protection. Of we-versus-them. A place where no one dares take risks. Where only the most naïve and uninitiated are optimistic about change, about the future, or about management competency. We would never confuse his world with a high-trust culture. Dilbert is the poster-boy for the trust-deficit syndrome.

We can't remove trust from the equation and expect stellar results in productivity and profitability.

Do any of us truly want to work in Dilbert's company? Could we reasonably expect his company to be blowing away the competition? Or chalking up new earnings records every quarter? Or setting the industry pace for profitability? How likely is it that Dilbert's company will ever win a J.D. Powers award for customer satisfaction? Or the Malcolm Baldridge Award for superior quality?

If we find such notions absurd, it's because we intuitively know that trust is vital. We can't remove trust from the equation and expect stellar results in productivity and profitability. Trust is power. Trust deficits, on the other hand, do nothing to empower us. They only impede us and pull us down.

9

Tributaries of Distrust

J ust as no one factor accounts for our trade deficit, there is no single cause of our spiraling trust deficit. It's like a mighty stream fed by dozens of tributaries, each one adding to the flow, making it broader, deeper, more robust.

In several instances, these tributaries of distrust rise well outside of the workplace. Their headwaters are far beyond our sphere of control as leaders. Nevertheless, these tributaries spill readily into our organizations and compound the challenge of trust-building.

Other sources of distrust spring from our own actions (or inaction) as managers and leaders. Here we have more control. In these instances we can attack the well-spring of distrust directly. And that's a primary objective of Trust-Centered Leadership™.

At the same time, Trust-Centered Leadership™ does its utmost to mitigate the impact of distrust flowing into the organization from outside. Thus, to have a full perspective of the trust-building challenge, we need a keen eye on all the tributaries that contribute to distrust, wherever these tributaries originate, whether within our organization or elsewhere. Seven tributaries are particularly important.

1. Societal Distrust. To some extent distrust in the workplace is a by-product of broad distrust everywhere in our society. In February 2002 a Harris poll found 78% of Americans agreeing with the statement, "I don't know whom to trust any more."[30]

Admittedly, the timing of this survey may have skewed the results. With the tragedy of 9-11 still dominating the national mood, we were learning to live with a patchwork of clumsy security measures, reminding us daily that even routine travel was no longer free of danger. The economic aftershocks of 9-11 were sending venerable industries into a tailspin. And in the midst of these unsettling events, corporate and clergy scandals grabbed daily headlines. It's no wonder that polls and surveys showed trust in short supply.

When there is widespread distrust of fundamental institutions in the American system, it is no surprise that distrust flows into the workplace.

There is little evidence, however, that trust has made a telling comeback since 2002. Another Harris poll, this one in January 2005, found that 62% did not trust the press; 77% did not trust political parties; 55% did not trust government; 70% did not trust big companies; and 51% did not trust labor unions.[31]

Religious and charitable communities fared better, with high approval ratings. But even there a third of the respondents did not trust religious institutions. And one in four did not trust charitable and volunteer organizations.

Significantly (especially for a nation of laws), forty-four percent expressed distrust of the judicial system. And this number may have actually understated the scale of this disaffection. Another Harris poll, six months later, put distrust of the legal system at

---

[30] Golin/Harris Poll, February 2002, *Trust,* ed. by James Lukaszewski.
[31] The Harris Poll #4, January 13, 2005, *Fewer Americans than Europeans Have Trust in the Media – Press, Radio, and TV.*

54%, with only 16% of the people expecting the system to protect them from frivolous legal claims.[32]

When there is such distrust of fundamental institutions in the American system, it's no surprise that distrust flows into the workplace. Workers need compelling reasons to see their company as strikingly different from other large institutions and organizations that they've learned to distrust.

2. Scandals. This general distrust in our society has been aggravated by scandals that have grabbed national headlines for over a decade. Enron is the classic, of course, along with Global Crossing, WorldCom, Adelphia, and Tyco, plus dozens of other companies who somehow managed to misstate revenues by billions of dollars or improperly backdate millions of dollars in stock options for CEOs and key executives.

Workers need compelling reasons to see their company as strikingly different from other large institutions and organizations that they've learned to distrust.

Equally disquieting has been the spate of scandals that have plagued the Catholic Church, costing it millions of dollars to settle judicial awards. Non-Catholic communions have had their share of shocking revelations, too, well-attended by full coverage in the media and press.

And then there's Washington, which seems to revel in a scandal per month. Within government only the judiciary has remained relatively unscathed by scandal. Nor does partisan finger-pointing seem justified. Corruption has seduced Republican and Democrat alike.

---

[32] Harris Interactive, June 27, 2005. *Americans Do Not Trust the Legal System*, found April 29, 2006 at http://www.cgood.org/society-reading-cgpubs-polls9.htm.

Unfortunately, most day-to-day Americans know business, institutional, and political leadership only through the lens of news coverage. Thus, when corporate scandals are rife, average workers are likely to generalize what they've seen in the media and question the credibility of all business leadership, including top executives in their own organization.

3. Cultural polarization. Ever since the rise of labor unions, the workplace has been frequently polarized between management and labor. Suspicions and distrust have run deep on both sides of this divide, as evidenced by the ugly rhetoric of labor disputes and strikes. Now, adding to this tension, is a broader pattern of polarization across our entire culture.

The favorite break room entertainment in many organizations is "reading between the lines" of company communiqués, seldom in a way that promotes and increases trust.

Some argue that America has never been through a period when we have been as polarized on so many issues as we are today. Our country has often had deep discord, of course, none more wrenching than our Civil War. And we've had bitter, ugly political campaigns for 200 years. But previous eras of polarization tended to coalesce around a single issue. Slavery. Protectionism. The gold standard. This or that war.

In contrast, today's polarization reigns everywhere. Polarization on moral issues. Social issues. Political issues. Constitutional issues. Camps are divided right and left. Consensus seems impossible. And media has packaged its content so that, to be heard, you must reduce your message to an attention-getting sound bite.

Moreover, the more stinging your attack, the more likely the prospect of your sound bite gaining air time. The day of reasoned, gentlemanly debate and discussion seems distantly past. In its place we have an age of talking points and talking heads, where the goal is not dialogue, but driving home your party's agenda. Spin, not clarity, is the purpose of public discourse.

As a result, polarization has permeated our cultural atmosphere with deep misgivings and distrust. And because distrust is so common in daily life, it spreads unabated into the workplace. When leaders make announcements, employees start speculating about the truth versus the corporate spin. After all, political and media spin-masters have conditioned people to think this way. Corporate communication is rarely taken at face value. The favorite break room entertainment in many organizations is "reading between the lines" of company communiqués, seldom in a way that promotes and increases trust.

4. Mergers and Acquisitions. The most feared words in corporate America today may well be, "Someone is interested in acquiring us." A friend of mine, after more than 15 years with a stable, industry-leading firm, saw his company bought out, only for the new company to be swallowed by another within six months.

Then, six months later the process repeated itself again, and this time he did not survive. Sixteen years of faithful, dedicated service, taking the tough assignments that no one else wanted, consistently outperforming his peers, only to be rewarded with a 90-day severance package. He was, as the British say, "redundant."

Everyone seems to know a dozen stories like this. Even if workers trust their present management to watch out for them, they can't say as much about the unforeseen buyer who may pop up at any moment. As employees know all too well, performance and loyalty won't mean a thing when they too become "redundant."

Some merger and acquisition consultants now tell clients to minimize the "adjustment time" after an acquisition by making all terminations within 30 days of the purchase. This means that workers will have no opportunity to prove themselves to the new ownership. They are reduced to a mere nameless element in some distant number-crunching exercise.

With merger mania showing no signs of abating, and with entrepreneurs purposefully creating fast-growth companies in order to sell them in only a few years, workers have little incentive to trust corporate promises to "do right by our employees."

The problem is even acute in privately held companies, where relationships between owners and employees have traditionally been comparatively strong. I find that employees in these kinds of businesses are now quick to believe that the owners are probably looking for a buyer, even when no such plans are afoot. And employees are equally quick to believe that the owners' primary concern is maximizing the price they get for the company, not protecting worker well-being. Needless to say, when workers give voice to these kinds of suspicions, trust takes a blow on the chin.

5. Lost job security. It may be hard to believe, but one of my clients has an employee who is about to retire with 45 years of service. Another client is moaning the loss of wisdom in a few months when several specialists retire, each with over 30 years in the company. To say the least, such stories are becoming as rare as palm trees on the moon.

Today's young people not only anticipate several job changes in adulthood, they expect to change careers several times, as well. For them that's merely part of reality today. Their generation accepts frequent career change as inevitable.

A slightly older generation, on the other hand, began their careers with different expectations. They set out with a vision of a long, steady career with a great organization, rewarded at the end with a comfortable retirement. Unfortunately, they found themselves at mid-career with their dream shattered.

While this generation has grudgingly accepted that times have changed, it still harbors a sense that it was somehow betrayed. As young aspiring workers, this cohort had never heard the word "down-sizing." Or the more awkward term "right-sizing." Much less the term "outsourcing." But they now know the bite of these processes firsthand. And they resent it.

Even when down-sizing is only a remote prospect, they feel anxious about job security. Because they are older, usually with more longevity and higher salaries, they fear being the first ones axed when cost-cutting starts.

And it's not just job loss they fear. It's also the prospect of lengthy unemployment. Realizing that few companies seek older workers as fresh hires, they anticipate a much longer term of unemployment for themselves than for younger counterparts.

Apparently their fears have a basis in fact. *Fortune* magazine had a cover article in May 2005 entitled, "Fifty and Fired." The accompanying story delved into the experience of several veteran managers who lost positions in their early to mid-fifties. Some of them needed several years to find another job. The article even referred to them as being on "permanent vacation."[33]

These men and women had platinum-quality resumes, impressive skills, and a record of solid achievement. All to no avail. Their age seemed an intractable obstacle. Needless to say, their experience bodes ill for any older worker, especially one who is put on the street with less impressive credentials.

I've rarely talked to a victim of "right-sizing" who felt the company's new size was the "right" one. The few exceptions are usually high-level managers who have exited with a generous severance package.

At the "worker bee" level it's a different story. There people are quick to point out inequities in the way lay-offs were done. Or to cite evidence that favoritism compromised the process. In a word, they leave disillusioned.

Once they have been through this disillusionment – and especially if they go through it a second or third time – workers understandably become more guarded in trusting upper management. Usually their distrust lies just under the surface, out of view and

---

[33] John Helyar, "Fifty and Fired," *Fortune* (May 16, 2005), pp. 78-90. Helyar notes, "Getting fired during your peak years has always been scary. You'd scramble for a few months, but you'd find something. Today it's different. Get fired and you scramble for years – and still find nothing."

easily missed. Yet it's there, ready to be pricked. Ready to erupt at a moment's notice.

As Robert Hurley has noted, "We have a crisis of trust today in part because virtually nobody's job is truly secure."[34]

6. Leadership Styles. Reading the management literature of the 1990s, one might have concluded that corporate leadership was moving decisively toward more participative, collaborative management styles. There were, indeed, dramatic examples of this very trend. But old-style, autocratic, do-as-I-say management styles are still alive and well. And often entrenched.

One might also expect (again based on the management studies of the 1980s and 1990s) that workers would not tolerate such heavy handedness. They would simply walk out rather than put up with it.

But the early years of the new millennium took us through an extended period in which workers did not feel that they had much freedom to walk away from their jobs. Downsizing, outsourcing, the dot-com collapse, and the impact of 9-11 all took their toll on workplace opportunities. Even before 9-11, search firms themselves were downsizing because they had so little business in the pipeline.

Moreover, the limited business that was coming to search firms tended to be narrowly focused. No longer were they being engaged to find a new member of some management team. Instead, they were being instructed to find someone with specific experience in a specific process with a specific product in a specific industry within the last two years. With so many managers hungry for work, companies believed they could be just this exacting in their criteria and still surface a slate of interested candidates.

In this world, with scores of replacements standing eagerly in the wings, any worker who had a job was eager to hold onto it, even if it meant putting up with leadership and management styles that bordered on unbearable. People simply put in their hours and be-

---

[34] Hurley, "The Decision to Trust," p. 57.

came (to use Senge's term again) compliant employees. They also became masters at masking their distaste for their management team and their distrust of the management system.

Managers meanwhile, understaffed and overworked after extensive downsizing and layoffs, were themselves putting in extraordinary hours. With so much on their plate and with workers feeling unable to quit, it was easy for managers to forego participative or collaborative decision-making. Consensus-building or management-by-walking-about simply took too much time. In its place managers often moved to an "I say, you do" style of communication.

The economic recovery of 2005 and 2006 began to renew workers' options. By the spring of 2006 those who had been tolerating relentless, long hours were starting to jump ship. Especially the ones who had suffered through the downturn by knuckling under to a heavy-handed corporate culture. Today, as job opportunities are much improved, authoritarian management is finding it difficult to hold onto employees long-term.

Yet, having fresh options does not mean that employees will soon forget their sense of powerlessness and frustration during the lean years. As I talk with them, many workers tell me that management showed its true stripes during the bad times by taking advantage of its workforce. Management is still resented for extracting those long hours. For managing only by the numbers. For holding every nose to the grindstone.

As a result, the "lean years" experience has convinced these workers that management is primary interested in their output, not in them personally. This, in turn, in turn, will feed their distrust of management for years to come.

7. Frequent reorganization and restructuring. For organizations to be quick and nimble, they must be able to restructure immediately without losing momentum. Yet, from what I've observed, restructuring is typically more given to a speedy process than to comprehensive communication. In the press for speed, managers often do an inadequate job of helping their organization understand the clear strategic purpose for reorganizing.

Without such understanding, those down in the ranks view reorganization as little more than change for the sake of change. To them restructuring and reorganizing begin to look like "flavor of the month" leadership.

A mid-level manager said to me recently, "Well, it has been 18 months since they threw the last reorganization at us. I guess we're overdue for the next one." At the heart of this statement, but left unspoken, is a perception that top management is operating somewhat willy-nilly, trying first this, then that.

Also implied are other questions that undercut trust. Does upper management truly have a firm grip on the rudder? Do they have a consistent, orchestrating vision? And what about their competence and business acumen – is it up to the task?

Workers tend to have the greatest trust in their immediate manager, the least in distant corporate leadership.

When reservations like these are running in the background, trust is already on the defensive. Frequent reorganization also creates another unintended impact on trust. In corporate settings trust is largely influenced by personal working relationships, which frequent restructuring disrupts.

Research indicates that workers tend to have the greatest trust in their immediate manager, the least in distant corporate leadership. Studies also suggest that genuine trust in a manager does not emerge until he or she has been in a post for six months or more.

When reorganization occurs repeatedly over comparatively short periods of time, this trust bond between workers and immediate managers never has time to gel. And without trust in their immediate manager, workers are unlikely to have high trust in the overall corporate culture.

Now, I'm not arguing against restructure and reorganization. To the contrary. I just led an international organization through this very process. There are times when restructure is strategically the right thing to do. But reorganization, done too often or without properly communicating its strategic purpose, merely opens the door to distrust.

These seven factors then (and others, as well) add daily to our trust deficit. Several of them, as we've said, are beyond the control of anyone in a given company. Yet their pressure is felt inside every corporate culture.

For this reason, organizations everywhere are vulnerable to distrust. When I picture this vulnerability, I imagine a West Texas sandstorm. No matter how much you try to seal your house against these beastly storms, they somehow manage to coat the inside of your house with a fine layer of dust. It creeps in through doorframes, cracks, windows, and any other unguarded place.

On other occasions I illustrate our susceptibility to distrust by borrowing from my days as a deck hand in the Navy. One of my jobs was to polish the brass work, stem to stern. It usually took several hours. Then, two days later, we would start the process again, for salt spray was already corroding the metal.

Like that fine dust carried by the sandstorm or the salt spray lofted by the ocean breeze, distrust is "in the air." It is part of the surrounding atmosphere, eager to creep in or grab hold wherever it sees opportunity.

That's why Trust-Centered Leadership™ never lets down its guard, even if trust is currently in a high state of repair. The brass work of trust may be bright and shiny today. But leave the proactive process of trust-building unattended, and trust can corrode overnight.

Part

2

Key Concepts for Building Trust

10

Defining Trust

I f you search the internet for quotes on trust, one humorous quip by Ron Nesen pops up on hundreds of sites. "Nobody believes the official spokesman," he notes, "but everybody trusts an unidentified source."[35]

Life, as Nesen reminds us, is a daily game of deciding which people to trust and how much to trust them. Seneca, the first-century philosopher, offers the same reminder when he says, "It's a vice to trust everyone, and equally a vice to trust no one."

Experts who study trust classify it under two headings. The first is interpersonal trust, the kind between husbands and wives, managers and employees, advisors and clients. Interpersonal trust allows us to confide our doubts to a friend. To lend our car to a neighbor for the weekend. To act on the advice of a mentor.

The second category is institutional trust, the kind that is tied to no one person in particular, but to a system, an enterprise, or an organization. Familiar examples include the trust we put in the air traffic control system, the monetary system, the judicial system, or the educational system. We also have institutional trust in the bank where we do our checking, the company that insures our house, the store where we buy our food.

Trust-Centered Leadership™ aims at enlarging both interpersonal and institutional trust. Or to put it another way, the goal of

---

[35] Ironically, sites that quote Nesen on this matter of "unidentified sources" leave him unidentified, apart from his name.

Trust-Centered Leadership™ is to maximize both the personal trust people place in their leader and the trust they have in the leader's organization.

When we talk about Trust-Centered Leadership™, therefore, we need a definition of trust that applies equally to individual leaders, leadership teams, and entire organizations. Here is the definition I find helpful:

> *Trust is complete confidence that a person or an organization will consistently do what is right in every situation.*

Note that trust is not merely confidence. It's *complete* confidence. Unwavering confidence. Unassailed confidence. When trust is fully mature, we might even describe it as *absolute* confidence. At this level of magnitude trust becomes existential, for it runs so deep in our inner being that it fires off instinctively, automatically, without us even thinking about it.

Within organizations such absolute trust is a rare and extraordinary achievement, although we do find it in high-risk professions among teams who daily put their lives in one another's hands. Absolute trust is more commonly found at a personal level, where it occurs primarily among family members and close friends and in high-stake relationships, such as those between patients and surgeons.

In addition, the high level of trust we place in surgeons is an example of the interplay between institutional and interpersonal trust. In surgery we commonly entrust our life to someone who is a relative stranger. (Following a heart attack in 2005, I went into emergency by-pass surgery within 15 minutes of meeting the doctor who would perform the procedure.) How is it that we place such great trust so quickly in a specialist whom we hardly know?

It's because of what some call a halo effect. When we have high trust in an institution – in this case, the medical community – we tend to bestow a halo of trust on its credentialed representatives. Our institutional trust translates into interpersonal trust.

This is why Trust-Centered Leadership™ focuses on building both interpersonal trust and institutional trust. The greater the institutional trust, the more readily those who represent the institution – the "official spokesman" in Ron Nesen's quip – have a cloak of credibility and trust thrown over their shoulders.

In high trust organizations this same halo effect works to the advantage of leaders who take on new positions. Because they were named to the post by a trusted system or organization, they benefit from the halo effect of the organization's implicit stamp of approval. This grants new leaders an initial level of trust they might not otherwise enjoy.

Unfortunately, the converse also holds true. In corporate cultures where distrust is widespread, leaders in new roles face an even greater challenge in creating interpersonal trust than would be the case elsewhere.

If an institutional halo effect exists at all, its influence is usually short-lived. Once people start building a "history" with a new leader, actions and conduct quickly supplant any halo effect in determining the degree to which the leader is trusted.

So it's naïve to depend on halo effects long term, or even to expect them at all. When they occur, it's clearly a plus for the new leader. The wiser approach is to presume that in any new leadership post, trust-building must begin afresh.

But more on this later. Our immediate purpose is to explore our definition of trust and examine implications of its wording. This, then, takes us to the term "complete." Trust, we have said, is complete confidence that an individual or an organization will consistently do what is right in every situation.

The word "complete" came into our language from a medieval term that meant "to be full." Implicit in the idea of being "full," of course, is the potential of being depleted. That's why I chose the term "complete" to describe the kind of confidence we can rightly call trust. "Complete confidence" means that while full trust pre-vails at the moment, it is subject to depletion.

Thus, the task of trust-building is never "complete" in the sense that there is no more work to be done. We must continually replenish trust. A lake filled to capacity seems full, but evaporation alone will require additional inflow if the reservoir is to maintain its depth.

Completely filling the reservoir of trust, then keeping it resupplied, are twin priorities in Trust-Centered Leadership™.

Similarly, even high-trust organizations have forces at work that can cause trust to evaporate. Completely filling the reservoir of trust, then keeping it resupplied, are twin priorities in Trust-Centered Leadership™.

A second vital word in our definition is "consistently." Whether we are speaking of interpersonal trust or institutional trust, both are built and maintained in the same way – by consistently doing what is right. But what constitutes "consistently"?

People occasionally use the word "consistent" to mean "more often than not." That's hardly the meaning in this context. Our definition of trust draws on the root concept of "consistent," which traces back to a Latin word meaning "to stand firm." Consistency, in other words, is steadfast dependability.

Which brings us to a third key term. Trust-building is about steadfast dependability in doing "what is right." There is purposeful ambiguity in this choice of words. "Doing what is right" can refer either to doing the right thing morally and ethically (character) or to doing those things that lead to proper outcomes (effectiveness).

In trust-building both meanings are in play. People place only limited trust in leaders with stellar character, but poor effectiveness. They are likewise guarded about trusting leaders who get striking results, but are known for glaring character flaws. Both character and effectiveness are essential.

Effectiveness (securing the right outcomes) means doing a cluster of things right, including:

- making sound decisions (a measure of competence)

- making technical and professional choices correctly (a measure of acumen and expertise)

- managing interpersonal relationships appropriately (a measure of emotional maturity)

- making adroit moves politically (a measure of organizational savvy)

- making the most important things happen (a measure of personal impact)

- achieving the most vital objectives (a measure of results)

Not all of these effectiveness factors are critical in forming trust between friends or members of a family. But in building trusted leadership they are all essential, each and every one.

Based on our definition of trust, then, there are three primary considerations that people use in deciding to invest complete trust in a leader:

- a character factor (doing the right things morally and ethically)

- an effectiveness factor (getting the right outcomes)

- and a consistency factor (holding steadily to patterns of character and effectiveness)

The final phrase in our definition ("in every situation") expands on the notion of consistency. To be trusted completely leaders must consistently do what is right and do it consistently across all contexts. No matter what the relationship. No matter how intense the pressure.

When we speak of consistency across all contexts, we are not referring to every possible situation in life. Whether leaders make wise judgments in their families or with their investments usually has little bearing on the trust they receive in the workplace. To gain and retain trust in the workplace, however, they must consistently demonstrate character and effectiveness in every situation that impacts their organization and its people.

The process of maintaining trust is an on-going interplay between the *expectations* and *exhibited behavior*. Those who are granting trust have certain expectations about the one they are choosing to trust. The one being trusted must exhibit behavior that conforms to these expectations. Trust is complete confidence (expectation) that an individual or organization will consistently do what is right (exhibited behavior).

To be trusted completely leaders must consistently do what is right and do it consistently across all contexts.

As we have noted, "doing what is right" is purposefully ambiguous. Behind this "doing" are qualities – character, competence, acumen, maturity, savvy, etc. – that are themselves invisible. They only become evident when expressed in action.

We might therefore consider exhibited behavior as the controlling determinant of trust, since in forming trust, people base conclusions about character, competence, maturity, and the like entirely on the leader's actions.

The unique power of the halo effect, which we discussed earlier, is that it bestows positive expectation (confidence) even without firsthand observation of the leader's actions. Expectation precedes exhibited behavior. For this reason, some would question whether "halo effect trust" is truly trust at all. They would argue that leaders stepping into a new role have only the hopes of their people, not their trust.

Whatever we call this halo effect – whether we describe it as "trust" or "hope" – it's the only phase of leadership in which confidence in the leader is independent of observed behavior.

When trust in a leader is still forming (separate and apart from any halo effect), exhibited behavior precedes expectation. That is, the leader's actions and attitudes (exhibited behavior) must bespeak trustworthiness before followers will respond with a degree of confidence (positive expectations about the leader) that leads to trust.

Once trust is established and solidified, expectation no longer needs to be built. It's firmly in place. Exhibited behavior now surrenders the lead position and takes on the role of validating that the expectation remains justified.

Thus, at every stage, trust in leadership is an interplay between the exhibited behavior of the leader and the expectation of those being led. The same principle holds true when we evaluate the trust leaders have in their people. The leaders trust is a function of how well worker behavior validates the confident expectation their leader has of them.

A high-trust organization is basically one in which there is thorough alignment between exhibited behavior and confident expectation in every working relationship. This alignment determines the degree to which

- people trust their leaders

- leaders trust their people and

- peers trust one another

11

Strong as Nails,
Fragile as a (Pete) Rose

W e've described trust as the glue that holds an organization together, especially in times of adversity. Indeed, it's
super glue, with a power to unite that is transcended
perhaps only by love and the bonds of family. Yet, despite all this
strength, enduring trust takes time to build and can be easily and
quickly lost.

Warren Buffet has noted that "it takes twenty years to build a
reputation and five minutes to ruin it." Charles Osgood once made
the same point in a clever bit of doggerel.

> One robin doth not a spring time make
> One swallow no summer at all.
> But I think I can state
> Without fear of mistake:
> One lark has caused many a fall.

Like trust, reputations are built and lost in two arenas of life.
One is the quality of our character. The other is how well we deliver. How well we perform. Because they are both linked to character and performance, trust and reputation tend to rise and fall together.

I'm speaking here of the reputation you have developed within
the organization you currently lead, not the reputation you brought
with you when you came to your post. People don't trust you be-

cause of the reputation you've gained elsewhere. They trust you based on what they have personally seen from you.

There are exceptional situations, to be sure, when leaders have such stellar, widely-heralded reputations that they are afforded an initial level of trust when stepping into new roles and positions. Yet, even in this kind of extraordinary circumstance, the initial level of trust has an extremely short shelf life.

As soon as leaders begin to interact with their people, as soon as their people have an opportunity see them in action and to monitor their exhibited behavior, any influence from the old reputation starts to wane. People are now forming their own independent judgments of the new leader, feeling no duty whatsoever to conform their opinions to some prior reputation.

The essential first step in gaining widespread trust is to develop a reputation for trustworthiness.

Within the group, individual opinions and judgments of the new leader may diverge at first. They typically do. But as divergence gives way to consensus a new "verified" reputation emerges. This new reputation may or may not conform to the reputation that preceded the leader. But this "verified" reputation is now the reality – the "verity," the truth – within which the leader must gain and maintain trust.

Because verified reputations become "the truth" for a leader's people, reputation inevitably plays a decisive role in determining how much trust leaders enjoy. In fact, the essential first step in gaining widespread trust is to develop a reputation for trustworthiness. A verified reputation.

This towering influence of reputation, more than anything else, distinguishes trust-building in leadership from trust-formation in personal relationships. Trust among friends, acquaintances, and colleagues derives from the quality of their one-on-one relationship. Reputation plays little, if any part.

Within organizations, however, few people have an opportunity to know their leader in anything more than a passing relationship. Their opinion of the leader – particularly when people are new to the organization – is almost exclusively a function of the leader's reputation and public persona.

Unfortunately, reputations have a powerful and influential life of their own, much of it outside the leader's control. Over time an unpredictable admixture of rumor, selective memory, speculation, misunderstandings, distortion, and suspicion color a leader's reputation.

All leaders face this hazard. But it's far more consequential for Trust-Centered Leadership™, since trust cannot escape unscathed whenever the leader's reputation is damaged. Therefore, for Trust-Centered Leadership™ the task of managing a proper reputation is never a task to be taken lightly or casually.

This is not to suggest some type of "image management" in the modern political sense of the word. The very artificiality of image management can work to destroy trust, not strengthen it.

Instead, reputation management is simply a determination to be proactive, and tirelessly so, in promoting a solid reputation. Since trust coalesces around reputation, a circumspect reputation is singularly essential to Trust-Centered Leadership™. When trust is lost, it's because of a failure (whether actual or perceived) to live up to expectations in either character or performance.

I've had leaders say to me, "I don't care a whit about what people think of me. I just want to get things done." Which is their way of saying, "I don't care if people like me or not. I'm going to do what I think is necessary."

On one hand this disinterest in winning a popularity contest is commendable in a leader. But reputation management is not about making oneself popular. It's about manifesting a quality of character and a level of effectiveness that makes it easy for trust to flourish.

Thus, while it may be workable in certain leadership contexts not to "care a whit about what people think," it's a deadly attitude for Trust-Centered Leadership™ and for the prospects of building a Trust-Based Organization™.

Leaders may not be able to control their reputation entirely, but neither are they powerless to keep it in good repair. To borrow a term from tennis, they can certainly prevent "unforced errors." They can avoid statements and behavior that discredit themselves needlessly.

They can also be vigilant to self-edit what they say and do. And when they realize even the slightest potential for a statement or action to be misunderstood or misinterpreted, they can waste no time in making timely clarifications before their reputation sustains inadvertent damage.

It's possible to lose a reputation for character without losing a reputation for performance, and vice versa. In baseball Pete Rose will always be celebrated as one of the most talented and successful players in the history of the sport. His performance was beyond dispute. But a flaw in his character cost him a place in the Hall of Fame.

In a similar vein, the chronicles of business are replete with stories of CEOs, men and women of stellar character, who take one company to the pinnacle of success, then move to another where they produce mediocre or even disastrous results.

Now their reputation for achievement is tarnished. And if they follow up with lackluster results in yet another CEO slot, they will no longer be trusted as leaders who perform, even though their character may be unquestioned.

For a leader whose goal is a High-Trust, Peak-Performance Organization, trust-building is not an either/or proposition in which a choice is made between building a solid reputation for character or else building a reputation for performance. It's about maintaining a genuine reputation for both, all the while recognizing that trust in both instances is fragile. One lark has caused many a fall.

What makes trust so fragile? How can it be so strong on one hand, yet so vulnerable on the other? The answer is found in two realities.

For one, trust develops at a measured pace, since the process depends on observation over an extended period of time. The observer needs this time to develop confidence that the other person is indeed characteristically trustworthy. During this period of development, trust may not be strong enough to bear a discrediting blow.

Trust's second vulnerability is its dependence on reputation. Reputation is always in the hands and hearts of other people. When people quit holding us in high repute, their trust in us declines.

Unfortunately, human nature is hard-wired in such a way that damage to reputations occurs with relative ease. Psychological research verifies that "negatives" have more power to change people's opinion of us than do "positives." You can validate this for yourself with a simple little experiment.

Ask friends to imagine that they have recently begun working with someone new at work. Then have your friends answer the following sequence questions.

First ask, "How many displays of genuine honesty will you need to see from this person before you conclude that your new associate is truly honest – honest enough that you would lend him fifty dollars without reservation?"

In responding to this question, some of your friends will answer with a specific number, or perhaps a narrow range of numbers. Others will avoid an exact figure, saying that they would need time to "get to know the person." They are saying, in essence, "The exact number is indefinite, but it's high enough that it won't be achieved in a limited period."

Now pose a second question: "Once you perceive this new associate as honest, how many acts of questionable honesty does it take for you to conclude that this same person is in fact dishonest?"

Answers to the second question will be distinctive in two ways. First, it will generally take fewer incidents – significantly fewer, as a rule – to destroy a reputation for honesty than it took to build the reputation initially. And second, people who avoided a numeric response to the first question are likely to be more specific with this one. And like everyone else you survey, they will also typically offer a number (or range of numbers) that is quite small.

Now put a third and final question to your friends: "Once you come to see this person as dishonest, how many acts of honesty will be required in order to restore his reputation for honesty in your eyes?"

People seize much more quickly on rumors or incidents that discredit trust than on actions that reinforce it.

The replies to this third question demonstrate that once a reputation for honesty is lost, restoring that reputation takes far longer than building it in the first place. In some cases, to be sure, a damaged reputation (and hence, damaged trust) may be irreparably damaged and thus unrecoverable.

Collectively the answers to these three questions reflect the relative weight of "negative" and "positive" incidents in shaping how others think of us. Indicators of dishonesty are clearly more powerful (it takes fewer of them to alter a reputation) than those that validate honesty.

What your experiment demonstrates about honesty is equally true of other trust-forming traits, according to research.[36] People seize much more quickly on rumors or incidents that discredit trust than on actions that reinforce it. And this leaves trust at the mercy of a process in which trust-formation is more easily damaged than maintained.

This disparity leads some researchers to refer to trust-building as an "asymmetric" process. One researcher who uses this term is Paul Slovic, who identifies four contributing factors that make it more difficult to build (or rebuild) trust than to lose it.[37] In summary, these are his conclusions.

- Events and actions which enlarge trust are typically less visible and noticeable than those which destroy trust. As a consequence, months of quiet trust-building behavior can be immediately overshadowed by one dramatic event that puts trust in question.

- Psychologically, when we become aware of negative events, they preoccupy us to a greater extent than do positive events. (This may be a natural defense mechanism which helps us be more highly attuned to potential threats than to things that pose no hazard.)

- Because of this proclivity toward the negative, we frequently give greater credibility to sources of bad news than to sources of good news.

- Distrust, once developed, tends to promote actions and attitudes that serve to deepen the distrust. As Slovic words it, "By avoiding others whose motives or actions we distrust,

---

[36] M. Rothbart and B. Park, "On the Confirmability and Disconfirmability of Trait Concepts," *Journal of Personality and Social Psychology*, 50, 131-142 (1986).

[37] Paul Slovic, "Perceived Risk, Trust, and Democracy," *Risk Analysis*, 13:6, 675-682, 1993.

> we never get to see if these people are competent, well-meaning, and trustworthy."

When viewed against this backdrop, it's easy to see why one lark can lead to a fall. Yet, not every lark has this grievous outcome. Had Pete Rose gambled only one time, he might well have been disciplined by his sport. But he would also probably be in the Hall of Fame today. It was the repeated pattern of behavior, and his deception to cover it up, that led to his demise.

We all know stories of men and women who stumbled terribly at some point, shattering their reputation for either character or performance, yet who rehabilitated their reputation and went on to pace-setting careers.

What then determines whether singular episodes of flawed character or non-performance result in shattered trust? Several variables go into the equation.

1. The egregiousness of the event. Falsifying a profit and loss statement typically delivers a more severe blow to trust than overstating the cost of a meal on an expense account. Or to cite another example, the public generally does not condemn white lies as seriously as it decries willful misrepresentations in sworn testimony.

2. The domain of the event. Character and performance are different domains of trust. In settings where ethics, principled judgment, and moral fiber are of paramount concern (e.g., managing trust funds in a bank), compromised integrity does more severe damage to trust than a slowdown in performance.

Conversely, in settings where performance is key (e.g., a company on the verge of collapse, with only weeks to turn things around), there will probably be more latitude for lapses in character than for failure to perform.

3. The consequences of the event. Lapses in character or performance that prove costly in terms of dollars, lives, or property loss have a more adverse impact on trust than failures or miscues with less consequential outcomes.

The public lost much of its trust in the Federal Emergency Management Agency (FEMA) following Hurricane Katrina. The damage to trust would have been far less significant, however, had the agency committed the same type of bureaucratic blunders in response to widespread range fires in remote, sparsely-populated sections of the American West.

4. The constellation of factors surrounding the event. The adverse impact on trust is considerably more telling if a misdeed or a failure to perform is then covered up through some type of wrongdoing. Or if, in the wake of a lapse in character or performance, the chosen response is to blame others rather than accept responsibility.

By the same token, in other situations the constellation of background factors may in fact expand the room for trust to maneuver. Workers may willingly make allowances for a manager whose child is battling the final throes of a terminal disease, so that they overlook statements, actions, or performance by the manager that might otherwise destroy trust.

5. The degree to which the event runs counter to core values. Had Pete Rose only had a gambling problem, professional baseball might well have ignored problems in his personal life. It certainly has done so for many other star performers with pressing personal issues. But the fact that he gambled on his own sport violated a core ethos within his profession and shattered respect for his character.

In the case of Pete Rose the core value was held collectively. In other situations leaders lose respect for their character by violating core values held by some, but not necessarily everyone around them. For instance, a manager who spews out a stream of steady vulgarities is likely to lose the trust of workers who consider such speech offensive, even though most people in the organization dismiss the behavior with a shrug.

6. The degree to which the event is predictive of future actions. We tend to generalize from specific details or observations. When there is a failure of character or performance, observers must decide whether to view the incident as an isolated event or as a foretaste of things to come. If they conclude that the incident was more than likely an isolated occurrence, trust can recover more quickly.

For leaders who are building High-Trust, Peak-Performance Organizations, or simply those whose goal is a culture of trust, it is essential to excel in both character and performance. The two are equally important. Even though we have talked about character and performance as separate domains of trust, they cannot be divorced in reality.[38]

They stand side-by-side in shaping a leader's reputation. They are like those twin stars that NASA telescopes have identified in the recesses of space, two massive solar bodies in a locked orbit with one another. They have an interdependent co-existence. Any wobble in the rotation of one affects the orbit of the other. The same is true with character and performance.

When my children were small, some of their favorite toys were Weebles, round-bottomed little characters who are weighted so that they pop back into an upright position when pushed to one side or the other. As the children played with these little figures, they would chant the Weebles advertising slogan which said, "Weebles wobble, but they don't fall down."

---

[38] Terry Bacon's research (which we will note later) leads him to conclude that the essence of trust-building in all relationships is character, "but in a business context it's also about competence." Terry Bacon, *What People Want: A Manager's Guide to Building Relationships that Work* (Mountain View, CA: Cavis-Black Publishing, 2006), p. 4.

Unfortunately, that's not always the case with reputations. Twin stars may develop a wobble and continue in orbit for light-years. Weebles may wobble, but keep standing. When character or performance starts to wobble, however, reputations – and the trust that goes with them – are always at risk. One lark still causes many a fall.

12

Trust Is Like
Dagwood's Sandwich

I clearly remember the first time someone said to me, "I don't trust you." Even though it happened decades ago, I can still see his face as he spoke, the courtyard in which we were standing, the people milling around us. I can still feel the warm summer sun beating down on my face. I was so taken aback that every detail of the scene is etched firmly in my memory.

I also remember my mind going instantly into a swirl. Hurriedly I tried to recall any interaction with the man in which I might have acted in poor character or violated my integrity. Yet nothing came to mind.

I was in a quandary, the same quandary I would see years later as I sat with Jeff, a coaching client who had been crushed by a 360 review. Out of 64 measurements on the review, he scored lowest in trust. Just as I had done in that sun-drenched courtyard, he was searching furiously to recall some terrible misstep that had cost him his reputation for integrity.

For me, fortunately, the misery was short-lived. My critic immediately added, "You don't seem to have had much tragedy in your life. So I'm not sure you've got enough experience with tough life issues for me to trust your judgment." In other words, it was not my integrity or character that was in question. It was my experience. The depth of my wisdom.

I can remember a huge inner sigh of relief when I realized that my character and integrity were not the issue. As a result, while I was taken aback by my experience, it did not crush me.

My client Jeff was not so fortunate. When he and I met, he was reacting to his review the way most of us do when told, "I don't trust you." He felt his character and integrity were being impugned.

And it was easy to see how he had reached this conclusion. The 360 review merged trust with integrity as a single category in reporting results. It therefore showed him scoring lowest in "Trust and Integrity."

Now, you should know that Jeff had a stellar record for building high-trust, high-performance teams in a number of large companies and in very high-stakes settings. He prided himself on these achievements and attributed much of his success to his constant vigil to maintain integrity. How, then, could this new team see him as deficient in character?

It would be weeks before we drilled down to the root of the poor ratings. And when we got there, it had nothing to do with Jeff's character.

He had been hired from the outside to implement sweeping change in the company's quality engineering program. He was basically charged with throwing out "the standard way of doing things" that had prevailed in the company for a generation.

Before Jeff arrived, however, upper management failed to communicate the compelling rationale for these changes. In effect the company merely hired Jeff, introduced him as the new quality guru, and announced that he would take the quality program in a new direction. Understandably, with no more explanation than this, Jeff's cohorts saw little need for the changes he implemented.

Very quickly distrust of the new program spread through the ranks. This distrust then attached itself to Jeff as the point man for the new system. It was neither his character nor his integrity that were in question. It was his agenda.

These two stories illustrate an often overlooked realty. Acting with character and integrity is only one aspect of building and maintaining trust. People do expect their leader to have integrity and strength of character, of course.

But their expectations run far beyond this one dimension of trust. Their performance expectations of leaders are multi-layered, like Dagwood's proverbial sandwich.

For instance, my critic in the courtyard trusted my character, but not my competence. With Jeff it was misgivings about his ultimate objective, not his integrity that fostered distrust.

More than a dozen character and performance expectations enter into the equation as people form trust in their leaders. (We will look at these expectations momentarily.) That's why the image of Dagwood's sandwich is so appropriate. Each of these expectations is a distinct layer of trust-building, just like the layers of ham and turkey and salami in his culinary concoction.

The job of trust-building is to match leadership performance to worker (or volunteer) expectations at each layer of the "trust sandwich." The more layers in which leaders perform well, the greater the trust they engender.

As a fan of alliteration, I challenged myself one day to find a word starting with "C" that could serve to identify each of these layers. So bear with my taste for alliteration in the list that follows.

1. Character. First and foremost, people expect character and integrity from their leaders. Strength of character is probably the most reliable predictor of how a person will behave, especially in trying circumstances.

The word "character" comes into English from a Greek term that described a die-cast used to stamp out coins. It literally means "what is stamped on a person." Coins, however, have no control over the image left behind once a die does its work. Debris in the recesses of the die will leave the coin permanently flawed.

Strength of character is probably the most reliable predictor of how a person will behave, especially in trying circumstances.

We, on the other hand, can overcome flaws in character. And leaders, above all others, must work to develop character which is thoroughly exemplary. Otherwise they not only impair trustbuilding, they lose the motivational power of leading by example.

2. Core Values. Character and integrity are inseparable from core values. For example, when we talk about people of integrity, we usually mean that their personal conduct squares with their core values. This assumes, of course, that we see their core values as appropriate. (Hitler's conduct, no doubt, squared with his core values, but his values were so despicable that few would describe him as a person of integrity.)

Beyond their tie-in to integrity, core values play at least two other critical roles in establishing leadership trust.

- First, to be fully trusted the leader's core values must align with the values most essential for executing the group's mission.

- And second, trust will be more readily granted when the leaders' core values (and the way these values are prioritized) are basically congruent with the prevailing core values among their people.

There are times, however, when we may want a purposeful mismatch between the values of leaders and the values of those they lead. This is especially the case when a malfunctioning or dysfunctional organization must be reformed. Reform often dictates an overhaul of values and value-structures.

Wholesale reform of this sort calls for leaders whose core values put them at odds with prevailing attitudes within their group. But whenever we create this type of intentional mismatch between leaders and their people, we must recognize that we have given trust a decidedly steep grade to climb.

3. Commitment. Core values determine commitment. We show very little commitment to values that are of peripheral importance to us. People therefore want to know that their leader is committed to them. To their cause. To their mission. To their well-being. And, as we have seen, to their values. They use evidence of the leader's commitment in order to determine how much he or she truly treasures what they treasure.

Leaders lose trust immediately, or may never gain it in the first place, if people conclude that their leader's commitments are primarily self-serving and self-aggrandizing. This accounts for the contrasting perceptions of politicians and statesmen. The former are perceived as watching out for their own career, first and foremost. The latter are viewed as always taking the principled course, whatever it costs them personally. As a consequence, while statesmen are generally respected and trusted, politicians are not.

4. Concern. We might easily classify a leader's concerns and commitments as two sides of the same coin. I've chosen to treat them separately because one particular area of concern is so vital to the enterprise of trust. When over 100 people from a variety of organizations were asked what led them to trust a manager, the second most frequent response was, "Someone who genuinely cares for me." [39]

Why did this factor figure so large in personal decisions to trust a manager? It probably has something to do with the kind of world in which we live, a world which excels at making people feel unnoticed, unvalued, and unimportant. Wherever we turn, we are

---

[39] Robert Galford and Anne Seibold Drapeau, *The Trusted Leader: Bringing Out the Best in Your People and Your Company* (New York: The Free Press, 2002), p. 39.

little more than another number. Another body in the queue. The workplace is so important to most people that they don't want to feel like another number there, too.

For this reason they look eagerly to their direct managers in hope of finding expressions and indicators of genuine concern. They also want to feel that their own concerns and input are understood, recognized, and openly received by those to whom they report.

When people believe that their leaders genuinely care for them, they are likely to allow leadership more latitude for miscues in other arenas of trust-building.

To word this another way, commitment is an expression of the will, concern an expression of the heart. People want their leader's commitment to them to be heartfelt, not commitment rooted solely in duty or management responsibility. When people believe that their leaders genuinely care for them, they are likely to allow leadership more latitude for miscues in other arenas of trust-building.

5. Credibility. Most people link integrity and credibility together in a simple formula, which reads: integrity creates personal credibility, lack of integrity destroys it. But this formula, while valid in principle, does not address another key component of credibility in building trust.

People may believe you are a person of integrity who would never misrepresent the truth to them. But they may also believe that you are honestly misinformed. Or that you are speaking about a subject on which you have inadequate know-how.

In other words, credibility entails more than merely being truthful. To build credibility, we must also convey a sense of expertise and authoritative knowledge. This is why leaders often increase their personal credibility by saying, "I don't know." People want to be able to trust the words that come from their leader's mouth. They would rather have a leader confess a lack of knowledge than to be left wondering if their leader really knows what he or she is talking about.

6. Competence. Since credibility includes a perception of being knowledgeable, judgments about credibility sometimes turn on the question, "Is this person competent?"

Competence is primarily a measure of expertise and authoritative knowledge. But it also includes the wisdom to apply knowledge appropriately. We've all known subject-matter experts with an exhaustive command of data and research, but whose skill at strategic or practical application languished.

To convey a sense of competence, leaders must manifest practical wisdom across a broad array of leadership functions. Obviously they must have technical command of the field in which they lead. But equally important is competence in dealing with people, in motivating them, in making effective presentations, in social graces, in defusing conflict, and in maneuvering political mine fields, just to name a few.

7. Concrete results. Nothing creates a reputation for competence more readily than impressive, concrete results. Leadership is not about good intentions. It's about execution.

During the Civil War, Abraham Lincoln was constantly frustrated with the failure of his generals to score decisive victories. The one exception was Ulysses Grant. When Lincoln announced his plan to put Grant in charge of Union forces, his cabinet objected.

"Mr. President," they argued, "Grant is a drinking man!" Lincoln is said to have replied, "Then find out what brand he drinks, and send a case of it to all of my generals."

In the final analysis character, core values, competency, and credibility amount to little if leaders do not achieve concrete results. This is why leaders in new assignments are well advised to focus on "low hanging fruit." To build trust, they need to establish a track record of solid results from the very start.

8. Convictions. Convictions are deep beliefs that you act on when you're under the gun. Do you believe that people are basically honest or dishonest? Lazy or industrious? Trustworthy or not? Does honesty really pay? Is personal transparency a good thing or a bad thing? Can I admit my mistakes without losing respect?

These questions, and dozens like them, shape our leadership style. These are not so much values as they are outlooks on life. They are filters through which we view the world. Thus, if I believe that people are fundamentally lazy, I will see abundant evidence to support my conclusion. And I will manage to ignore evidence to the contrary.

Convictions inevitably bleed through into attitudes. By monitoring our attitudes, people can usually surmise what our convictions are. To be trusted, leaders must display convictions that indicate respect for the people they lead, since none of us readily trusts a person who treats us with disrespect.

9. Control. A key function of leadership is to exercise a stabilizing influence in unsettled or unsettling times. People quickly lose trust for a leader who lets things get out of control. At the same time, they resent a leader who is overly controlling. The challenge for leaders, then, is to maintain control without becoming, in popular parlance, "a control freak."

In addition, leadership is exercised within a broader environment where many forces are beyond the leader's control. Often these forces constitute threats to the leader's people. People expect their leader to keep them safe from serious threats. When they conclude that the leader is not up to this job, they start rescinding their trust. Feeling safe, as we shall see, is a fundamental requirement for trust.

Leaders who are insecure also make a frequent mistake related to control and trust. Wanting to project an image of having substantial clout, they make promises and commitments about things over which they have little control.

One of two things then follows, and both are destructive to trust. Either the promises and commitments go unfulfilled, undercutting confidence in the leader. Or people recognize that the leader is exaggerating what he or she can deliver, which impales the leader's credibility.

10. Consistency. As we saw in exploring the definition of trust, consistency ranks alongside character, integrity, and performance in building trust. Consistency has many dimensions. Consistency between our words and our actions. Consistency in the way we treat people. Consistency in our behavior. In the way we manage our emotions. And in the way we apply policies. In addition, people need to see that their leader maintains this consistency from one context to another.

Consistency is a prime ingredient in predictability, a cornerstone of trust-building. People know how to relate to a leader who is consistent and predictable, even if the leader's style is far from ideal. What leaves them confused is a leader who is unpredictable. The resulting confusion then leads to uncertainty, and uncertainty spreads distrust. Not just distrust toward the leader, but toward the entire organization.

From a larger perspective, building a Trust-Bonded Organization™ calls for consistency in leadership styles and leadership priorities at every level of management. Recognizing this, one of my clients, a Fortune 200 company, has devoted immense energy and investment to using their Leadership Model, developed by their senior executive team, as the primary focus for all of their internal mentoring and leadership development programs.

The result is exceptional leadership alignment far down into the organization. And this alignment has been instrumental in keeping trust in good repair in one of the most schedule-intensive companies in the world.

11. Carry-through. Closely akin to consistency is carry-through. Failure to carry through can range from dropping the ball altogether to regularly missing promised deadlines. Carry-through boils down to the simple practice of doing *what* you say you will do and doing it *when* you say you will do it. Failure to carry through skewers credibility and leaves trust tattered.

At the corporate level carry-through often takes the form of aligning rewards and promotions with announced initiatives. I consulted one of the nation's largest banks a few years ago as they implemented a strikingly new approach to marketing loans. But loan officers who bought into this initiative soon learned that performance reviews, bonuses, and promotions were going to people who were still doing things the old way.

Not surprisingly, the initiative ultimately failed. Moreover, the failure created an atmosphere of skepticism and distrust which greeted other new initiatives in the future.

Corporate consistency also means sticking with change initiatives for the long haul. The Fortune 200 company that I mentioned above not only announced a Leadership Model that would anchor their leadership development program, they have persisted in that plan year after year.

As a result, no one views the Leadership Model and the internal mentoring program as some passing fancy or momentary fad. People take the model seriously. They now firmly believe that by embracing the model and following it effectively, they secure a promising future within the company.

12. Clarity. Leaders are expected to communicate both vision and a plan for translating the vision into concrete results. This means that they must first have clarity themselves on what needs to be done. And second, they must communicate these needs in terms that are clear, crisp, and precise.

Clarity is the requisite first step in knowing where we need to go. Clarity begins with properly understanding the current situation and its urgencies. In leadership communication one of the primary goals is to create a shared perspective of
- where we are
- where we need to go
- how we will get there, and

- how we will know when we've done well

Leaders thus use communication to demonstrate that they have properly sized up the situation and have a cogent, workable plan of action. One of the most lethal trust-busters is for workers to conclude that their leaders are clueless. When workers start saying, "Management doesn't have a clue," trust is losing its foothold.

Trust also makes a speedy exit when leaders fail to communicate expectations and assignments with such clarity that those who are given directives know clearly

- what is expected
- when it is expected
- how they are expected to do it, and
- the form in which it is expected

Nothing shatters confidence in a leader more quickly than for a worker to put in countless hours fulfilling an assignment, only to be rebuffed at the end with, "That's not what I wanted at all!"

When workers start saying, "Management doesn't have a clue," trust is losing its foothold..

As a rule, managers don't blame themselves for these breakdowns in communication. They hold the worker accountable for not listening. But the worker will beg to differ. The worker will believe that he or she did indeed listen carefully and did everything reasonable to meet expectations.

From the worker's perspective the rebuff for not listening is unwarranted and serves only to indicate incompetence on the part of the leader, who is now seen as fickle and capricious or else either too incompetent or too lazy to give instructions clearly. None of these conclusions, obviously, fosters trust.

13. Counsel. Over the past 20 years we have seen significant shifts in how the role of leaders is defined. Today we frequently describe leaders as mentors and coaches, a concept virtually unheralded a generation ago. Contemporary leaders today are expected to be people who can offer wise counsel and ask probing insightful questions. This is in addition to the career counsel that leaders have long been expected to provide as part of periodic employee reviews.

Because these coaching-mentoring-career guidance conversations carry such high stakes for the employee, workers typically take them seriously. If workers lose confidence in their leader's counsel, they will typically then move on to question the leader's competence and credibility, which delivers a telling blow to trust.

14. Candor. We live in the age of spin, word-smithing, and artful euphemisms. We've learned to be suspicious of statements from leadership circles. We scour official pronouncements, not only for what they say, but equally for what they avoid saying.

In this climate of suspicion, people are quick to label a leader's comments as spin, even when they are not. Simply by donning the mantle of leadership, today's executives and managers step into a role where the credibility of their public statements is held up for unprecedented scrutiny.

Candor – being forthright, to use a somewhat outdated term – is thus vital to building trust. With today's technology, people can instantly check out the veracity of leadership statements. And they will.

Once workers conclude that they are being subjected to straight-faced spin, they will feel insulted, to say the least. To them the strategy of spin is evidence of a demeaning management attitude. Either management must believe them too stupid to see through the charade. Or else management is saying to them (to quote Jack Nicholson's famous line in *A Few Good Men*), "You can't handle the truth!"

Either way, trust is lost. And now another problem is added to the mix. Few things irk people more than being treated as stupid or incompetent. Yet, this is precisely the way persistent spin leaves workers feeling. Needless to say, they will not repay such insult with either loyalty or trust.

In listing these elements of trust, I have struggled with how best to sequence them. Whenever we present a list in a one, two, three fashion, we run the risk of suggesting that the more important items occur highest in the list.

Let me say, therefore, that there is no prioritization in the arrangement that I've selected. Lost candor, at the end of the list, can be as damaging to trust as questioned commitment near the top. In addition, these trust-building elements work in concert with one another, so that none of them is isolated in terms of impact from the rest.

My sole purpose in providing this list is to demonstrate that leaders must pursue trust-building purposefully and simultaneously at many different levels of interaction with their people. (When building his sandwich, Dagwood doesn't care whether he adds ham first or salami first, just so long as both are in the stack.)

Trust is not solely a matter of integrity and credibility. Trust-building is a complex, multi-layered endeavor, becoming more complex with every passing year. And it deserves as much strategic focus as any other aspect of leadership responsibility.

As one team of researchers has said, "It takes more than personal integrity to build a trusting, trustworthy organization. It takes skills, smart supporting processes, and unwavering attention on the part of top managers."[40] They add that "trust within organizations is far more complicated and fragile" than trust between individuals. That's why wise leaders pay attention to every level of trust-building within their organization.

---

[40] Robert Galford and Anne Seibold Drapeau, "The Enemies of Trust," *Harvard Business Review* (February 2003), p. 89.

13

Guiding Principles of Trust-Centered Leadership

E verything I've learned about Trust-Centered Leadership™ traces back to a simple but profound realization: It's the recognition that trust only exists because someone chooses to grant it.

You cannot demand trust. You cannot mandate it. And despite our language to the contrary, you can't even earn it. Trust is something that others bestow on you. It's their choice, not yours. Trust, like beauty, is in the eyes of the beholder.

Don't rush past this concept. Take time to ponder it, because it's replete with implications. For example, think about what's implied when we say that trust is conferred by the ones being led.

Trust, like beauty, is in the eyes of the beholder.

This means that trust in your leadership is always at the discretion of others. Workers are fully empowered to dictate how much leaders are trusted, or even if they are trusted at all. Workers are equally empowered to withdraw trust once it has been bestowed. This is one arena in which your people are fully, 100% empowered. And no corporate decision can revoke their empowerment.

It then follows that as a trusted leader, you must see yourself as the beneficiary of trust, not its progenitor. In the final analysis, you can't make trust happen. The trust you enjoy as a leader exists solely at the discretion of other people.

This reality has been implicit in every chapter thus far. Nowhere to this point (nor in the pages to come) do I speak of the leader creating trust. Leaders may do things to foster a trust-friendly atmosphere. They may nurture a climate conducive to enlarging trust. But they can do nothing to earn trust. Not in the strictest sense of the word.

When I present this concept, it occasionally triggers vocal objection. "Of course you can earn trust!" my objectors claim. They then recount things that they have done to deserve trust. But *deserving* and *receiving* are two different things. It's one thing to think I deserve a raise, quite another to get it!

Now, admittedly, we do sometimes say things like, "I earned a raise, but they didn't give it to me." In statements like this, "earned" and "deserved" mean basically the same thing. But when I talk about "earning trust," I'm speaking about actually receiving it. I call it "trust accounting on a cash basis." Let me explain.

Think of two profit-and-loss statements, one generated on an accrual basis, the other on a cash basis. If you are using an accrual system, income shows up on the P&L as soon as you are entitled to payment. The timing of the transaction is determined by your own action, such as submitting an invoice.

By contrast, income does not appear on the second P&L (the cash basis statement) until funds are physically in hand. In this system it's no longer you, but the party rendering payment whose action determines when the transaction posts.

Now let's return to my objectors. If you think of trust as something you accrue, the objectors have a point. Once you've done what it takes to deserve trust, you've "earned" it, in a sense.

But balances in accrued assets are phantom funds. You can't disburse them to make payroll. And when the going gets tough, "phantom trust" won't help you at all. To draw on your "trust" ac-

count, there must be funds on deposit. And deposits only occur
when people decide to place trust in you.

That's why I argue that trust itself cannot be earned. The deposits in a leader's trust account are always made by others, never
by the leader personally. And these deposits do not result from people feeling an obligation to their leader, as though they "owe" their
leader trust the way a customer owes a balance. The deposits are
the product of a willing decision to yield power and control to the
one being trusted.

The realization that trust is bestowed, not earned, accounts for
a unique thread that runs through the principles of Trust-Centered
Leadership™. These principles, one and all, assume that you are
not looking at the enterprise of trust-building from your perspective
as a leader, but from the perspective of those you lead.

This shift in perceptual position is indispensable. By getting
outside of yourself and taking the perceptual position of your people, you look at your leadership from the vantage of the ones who
control the trust-vote.

When you change your perceptual position, you are likely to
make a powerful discovery. You will find that your people view your
leadership against an altogether different backdrop from the one
that frames your own perspective. From your own perceptual position you see your leadership against your own experiences,
achievements, and proven track-record over your entire career.

When your people look at your leadership, they see very little of
this. From their perceptual position the backdrop for your leadership is their own history – their history with the organization, with
its leaders, and even with former employers. For good or ill, your
leadership plays out in the minds of your workers against the backdrop of their own resume and experience, not yours.

Thus, to practice Trust-Centered Leadership™ you begin by
looking at the challenge of trust-building from the perspective of
your people. From their vantage point, what are impediments to

trust that must be addressed? And not just impediments to trust in you as a leader. What are the impediments to trust among peers within the group? Toward management in general? Toward their internal and external customers? And what stands in the way of a greater atmosphere of trust across the entire organization?

Armed with insight from the employee's perspective, you are then prepared to make clearer judgments about how your actions and the actions of others are affecting trust. Are these actions creating an open invitation to trust? Or are they ripping the invitation to shreds? With this clarity, it's then possible to develop specific strategies for negating the impediments, or at least reducing their impact, and giving trust a friendly atmosphere in which to bloom.

If we cannot earn trust, then the corollary follows that trust doesn't come with your title. People aren't going to trust you just because you're the manager. Or the VP. Or the new president of the college. Trust will come later, after you have a track record with your people. After trust has had time to build.

Studies indicate that it takes six to nine months before people trust a new manager.

New managers commonly make the mistake of implementing sweeping changes immediately after taking office, thinking they must do so while they still enjoy high trust. The truth is, unless their people have known them and worked with them in the past, new managers and executives have very little trust at first. And premature, disruptive change may jeopardize what trust they do have.

Whenever possible, it's preferable to postpone wholesale or disruptive change until trust is established. Sometimes, however, extensive change can't wait for trust to build. Studies indicate that it

takes six to nine months before people trust a new manager.[41] Nine
months is an eternity in today's hyper-competitive world. Increasingly new leaders must take unpopular initiatives immediately,
without time to gain their people's trust.

When faced with this situation, the fall-back position for Trust-
Centered Leadership™ is to choose a change methodology that
keeps the potential for trust-building high. This means going the
extra mile to get input from your people before implementing
change. Help them feel assured that they are being heard and have
a voice in shaping your decision.

Then follow your decision with extraordinary effort to communicate the purpose, necessity, and benefits of the change. Not just
once. But repeatedly. Whenever possible, clearly identify the benefits to the workers in terms of their personal interests. Show them
specifically how this change is going to make their work more man-
ageable. More productive. More fulfilling.

These steps will help your people recognize that their new
leader is genuinely interested in them, their opinions, and their
well-being. Remember, having "a leader who cares for me" is one of
the most powerful trust-builders available to management. Thus,
Trust-Centered Leadership™ always makes change – particularly
in the first weeks of a new executive or management position – in
ways that convey genuine care and concern.

Just as trust does not come with the title, neither does it transfer with you from one leadership role to another. Trust is contextual. Being trusted implicitly in one setting may have little bearing
on the trust you enjoy in another. You may be a great mechanic,
and I may trust you implicitly to overhaul my car. But I probably
won't trust you to take out my appendix!

---

[41] When 215 company executives were asked how long it takes for them to
build trust in a new leader, the average response was seven months. Ironically,
they said it takes only three months for a leader to lose their trust.

I was making this point in conversation one day with a long-time executive at Southwest Airlines. He chuckled in agreement and said, "Yep, that's one lesson I learned the hard way."

He then related how he had spent 18 years in the company's finance department, mostly in top management positions. During this tenure he compiled an exceptional reputation for effectiveness and integrity. As the company positioned him for a senior executive role, they moved him into another functional area to gain broader knowledge of airline operations.

"Because I had been so trusted and respected in my old job," he said, "I just assumed that I would be trusted in the new one." Within a month, however, he had tossed that assumption aside. He discovered that the task of trust-building had to begin afresh.

Is this always the case? No, not necessarily. But in my experience, it's true more often than not. Trust-Centered Leadership™ always approaches a new leadership post presuming that trust must be built from the ground up. And it starts the building process from day one.

Our job as leaders is to conduct ourselves with such consistency and integrity that we make it easy for people to invest their trust in us.

This is another way of saying that resumes don't confer trust. Young leaders are especially prone to count on impressive academic backgrounds or a history of success in the right companies or in the right assignments to give them instant trust and credibility. It simply doesn't work that way.

One of my mentors used to say, "Your resume is only your union card. It shows that you hold the requisite credentials to be at the table. But once you're at the table, the union card doesn't mean a thing. From then on it's performance that counts."

Since trust is bestowed, not earned, our job as leaders is to conduct ourselves with such consistency and integrity that we make it easy for people to invest their trust in us. When I stepped onto campus in my new role as president, nothing in my resume or experience suggested that I could reverse its fortunes. I brought no magic wand. No bank vault filled with new funding. Certainly no track record at turning similar institutions around.

But what I did bring was a solid reputation, well known on the campus, for getting things done and shooting straight with people. That made it easier for critical constituencies to trust me. Their trust was my power. Truth be told, their trust was the only real power I had.

When I recognized that my power was entirely dependent on their trust, it led me to start examining the relationship between trust and power in general. Power comes in two forms. The power to coerce. And the power to influence. We see this difference in our distinction between those who *have* authority (such as a judge) – and with it the power to coerce – as opposed to those who *are* an authority (such as an expert witness), who have the power to influence and persuade.

In organizations, individuals with reputations for being authoritative in their knowledge can have far-flung influence even without positional power. Their judgments and opinions hold great sway because everyone views their know-how as authoritative and trustworthy.

Some researchers label this power to exert influence as authority, but hesitate to call it power. They narrow the definition of power to govern only situations in which one party is in a position to coerce others. Since influence is not coerced, but derived from trust in someone's reputation or wisdom, these researchers see influence as conferring *authority* but not *power* within an organization.

I prefer to avoid this kind of distinction, largely because popular speech frequently uses the word "authority" to denote people with coercive power, such as when we speak of police or military authority. It makes for clearer communication, I feel, to avoid a narrow definition of power, so that we speak of both the power to coerce and the power to influence.

Viewed this way, the decision to trust is in effect a power transaction. Those who trust are choosing to forego a certain degree of their own power and control, "entrusting it" to someone else.

An outside observer might have thought that my power as president of the college was invested in me by the board. And that would be true, if we are speaking of coercive power. As president I was fairly free to hire and fire. To slash budgets. To restructure staff.

But given the circumstances, I had very little coercive power, regardless of my title. With payrolls unpredictable, I had almost no financial leverage over staff and employees. And while I did have the power to dismiss, it was toothless power. How likely was I to find a qualified replacement when our circumstances were so perilous?

To the degree that I had genuine power, then, it was not the power vested in me by the board, but the power granted to me by a community of people who gave me their trust. I call this "trust-based power" as opposed to positional power.

Potentially the most effective leaders are those who combine positional power with trust-based power. Trust-Centered Leadership™ aims at yielding this very convergence. Positional power comes with your title. Trust-based power comes from your people.

In Trust-Centered Leadership™, therefore, it's imperative to habitually step outside of your own perceptual position and view things from the perspective of others, asking yourself, "What can I do that will make it even easier for people to invest their trust in me?"

When we start asking ourselves this question, we must also confront the issue of whether we as leaders truly trust our own people.

It's human nature to trust those who trust us. When we do not trust our people, our non-verbal communication tends to signal our distrust. People will pick up on these signs of distrust and reciprocate in kind.

Terry Bacon, founder and CEO of Lore International Institute and one of America's veteran executive coaches, surveyed 500 people in a variety of industries to determine what they most wanted from their managers and their workplace. His study, conducted from 2004-2005, identified trust as the thing workers want most. In summarizing the results, Terry notes that trust "ranked at the top of virtually everyone's list of needs."[42]

Micromanagement and managing through intimidation are two of the most common ways in which leaders communicate distrust of their people. Both micro-management and intimidation are a way of saying, "I can't trust you to do what is right unless I ride herd on you."

Micromanagement and managing through intimidation are two of the most common ways in which leaders communicate distrust of their people.

As I'm coaching senior executives, I routinely ask, "How much do you trust the people below you?" Often they have to pause to think about the question. They have thought frequently about whether they trust management above them. But they have given less consideration to their trust of their own workforce.[43]

---

[42] Terry Bacon, *What People Want,* p. xviii.

[43]There are relatively few published studies on how a leader's trust of his or her subordinates impacts both the leader's performance and the overall performance of the organization. One study which has looked into this subject is Kristin L. Strater, "The Effects of Supervisors' Trust of Subordinates and their Organization on Job Satisfaction and Organizational Commitment," *International Journal of Leadership Studies* I, No. 1, found March 26, 2007 at http://www.regent.edu/acad/sls/publications/jounals/ijls/new/vol1iss1/editor/fields.htm.

Intriguingly, more than once I have had managers say, after a lengthy pause, "You know, I'm not sure I trust my people all that much." And having made that realization, they are then in a better position to understand why they are sensing distrust from those they lead. Their own distrust of their people is generating reciprocal distrust by way of response.

If we want our people to trust us as leaders, we must begin by trusting them and communicating our trust both verbally, non-verbally, and through our actions. Once leaders acknowledge to me that they don't trust their people, my next query is, "What needs to be different in order for you to trust them?"

I've learned not to anticipate the answer to this question. The reply is sometimes as simple as, "I guess I don't trust them because I don't know them very well. I think if I just spent some time getting to know them, trust wouldn't be a problem."

Sadly, the barriers to trust are not always so easily remedied. In explaining why they distrust their people, I've had leaders question the very integrity of their workers. Or their team's work ethic. Or their employees' attention to standards of performance. When these are the kinds of barriers that prevent leaders from trusting their people, it will take time, effort, and investment to overcome the obstacles to trust. But they must be overcome.

Indeed, once the obstacle is identified, my next question is, "What is your action plan to remove the barriers that stand in the way of your trust?" Putting this action plan into effect is essential, since a leader who is unable to trust his or her people is unlikely to ever gain their trust in return.

Admittedly, the reasons for distrusting our people are sometimes justified. Early in my presidency at the college I discovered some sizable "plug entries" that had been used in two consecutive years to balance the books.

I was well-acquainted with the person who made these entries, and with the accountant who had sanctioned them. I had no reason in either instance to be suspect of their basic integrity. But it was apparent that they had resorted to plug entries because they could not otherwise find a way to reconcile the account balances.

Now, without question, they were dealing with some very extraordinary issues that made an end-of-year reconciliation extremely difficult. But given our financial nightmare, I needed to know that I could trust our financial statements down to the penny.

In situations like this, faced with legitimate reasons for distrusting a worker's competency in a vital skill area, two questions become important for us as leaders. First, do we trust the person's potential to overcome the skill limitation, perhaps through further training or coaching? If not, our only choice is either dismissal or reassignment.

On the other hand, if we believe the limitation is surmountable, the next question is, "Do we have time to wait for the additional skill or work habits to develop?" If not, again we must choose between dismissal or reassignment.

This is exactly the conclusion I had to reach with these two people. Whatever their potential to become more adept, our financial crisis was too pressing and too immediate for me to have the luxury of a developmental timeframe. So I made two of the most difficult dismissals of my life, for they were both good friends and had supported me solidly as the campus leader.

But let's consider the other alternative. Let's imagine a situation in which we believe 1) that our people have the potential to master new skills and work practices and 2) that we have time to wait for them to develop.

This confidence is itself a form of trust. It is not so much trust in what they do at present as it is trust in what they may become in the future. (If I don't have this type of confidence in their future, either something is wrong with my action plan to develop my trust in them, or else I should have moved to dismiss or reassign them rather than try to retool them.)

While our people are developing these new work attributes, we must communicate our trust in their potential just as congruently as we would like to be able to communicate our trust in their performance. Again, people will pick up intuitively on our trust (or distrust) in them.

If we cannot say forthrightly that we trust their skills, abilities, or work habits, we need to communicate the trust we do have. Your people are not likely to trust you more than you trust them.

Your people are not likely to trust you more than you trust them.

Earl Graves, whose many businesses include *Black Enterprise* magazine, writes, "Trust brings out the best in people. If they sense they are trusted, they will rise to the occasion." He then tells how he learned this truth while serving on Robert Kennedy's staff.

> [Kennedy] had absolute trust in the folks working for him, and we responded to that trust by doing everything we could to live up to his expectations. He could have said to his staff, "I'd like to play basketball in the office tomorrow," and we would have set to work that evening raising the ceiling, putting in a hardwood floor, and setting up the nets. That's the kind of dedication, engendered by trust, every manager dreams of.[44]

With an eye to creating that same depth of dedication, then, let's bring this chapter to an end by summarizing the critical presuppositions and principles of Trust-Centered Leadership™ that we have examined thus far.

- Trust is bestowed, not earned.

---

[44] Daisy Wademan, "The Best Advice I Ever God," *Harvard Business Review* (January 2005), p. 43.

- Trust comes from performance, not your title.

- Trust is contextual, which means that trust-building must begin afresh with every new leadership assignment.

- Trust is transactional, a transaction in which your people willingly transfer power and control from themselves to you as their leader.

- As a leader, the first step in facilitating this transfer is to adopt the perceptual position of your people and identify, from their perspective, the impediments to trust that must be addressed.

- Leadership has its greatest potential when it combines positional power with trust-based power.

- Leaders must trust their people if they expect their people to trust them.

With those principles before us, we turn next to the process of developing a culture of trust.

3

Building a High Trust Culture

14

Two Formulas for
Creating a Culture of Trust

T
he primary objective of Trust-Centered Leadership™ is to create a culture of trust. This means developing an environment in which high levels of trust govern every relationship in your organization, as well as the relationship between your organization and its external and internal customers.

The more fiercely competitive your marketplace, the more critical it is to have a culture of trust in order to maintain sustainable competitive advantage. Without a culture of trust, no company will ever rival Jack at being quick and nimble.

Kathleen Ryan and Daniel Oestreich, long time researchers on threats to workplace trust, have concluded that when organizations perform well, it's "not because job descriptions are well thought and explicit." Instead, it's "because of the quality of relationships between people."

Human resource systems are important, they add. But "they can never be a substitute for energizing, trust-based relationships at the heart of an organization that is meeting the challenge of the new era."[45]

---

[45] Kathleen D. Ryan and Daniel K. Oestreich, *Driving Fear Out of the Workplace: Creating High-Trust, High-Performance Organizations* (San Francisco: Jossey-Bass, 1998), p. 47.

Leaders are forever engaged in a "culture war" against in-grained patterns of work, behavior, and attitudes that run counter to a culture of trust. Understandably, the more trust we amass as leaders, the more leverage we have in this "culture war," for a high-trust culture never matures without trusted leaders.

On the other hand, I am not suggesting that we should postpone engaging in the "culture war" until we ourselves are fully trusted as leaders. That's neither necessary, nor even wise. The two objectives – gaining trust in ourselves as leaders and developing a culture of trust around us – can be and should be pursued in tandem.

Indeed, the two are intertwined. People are less likely to trust you personally if building a culture of trust seems only secondarily important to you. Conversely, the more they trust you as their leader, the more likely they are to help you transform the culture.

———————————

A culture of trust radiates an emotional energy field that pulsates with confidence, openness, dedication, collaboration, creativity, and loyalty. Our role as leaders is to foster an atmosphere (what chapter four calls a "climate of trust") in which this kind of positive emotional energy cascades freely through our organization.

For the balance of this book I want to examine how to generate this kind of energy field. Our focus will be on two formulas, each in the form of an acronym and each one structured around elements that are vital to a Trust-Bonded Organization™.

The first acronym, what I call the SIRVU formula, highlights five basic assurances that people must feel in order for trust to take root. In general trust will flourish in any culture only to the degree that people feel

- Safe
- Informed
- Respected
- Valued
- Understood

Note the operative verb "feel." To have a culture of trust, people must *feel* safe, informed, respected, valued, and understood.

This requires much more than a simple resolve by leadership to protect and inform people, to respect and value them, and to make determined efforts to understand them. These kinds of leadership commitments are necessary, to be sure. But they are not enough.

To cultivate a culture of trust, leaders must foster an environment where everyone – leader and worker alike – is committed to treating others in ways that make the SIRVU assurances universally felt.

From the SIRVU formula we then move to the HI-TRUST formula, which spells out seven qualities that people must see in their leaders in order for trust to mature. These seven are

- Humility
- Integrity
- Truth
- Responsiveness
- Unblemished Fair Play
- Support and Encouragement
- Team Care

Together the SIRVU and HI-TRUST formulas address the four critical arenas (introduced in chapter four) in which Trust-Centered Leadership™ pursues "trust-friendliness": Climate, Character, Conduct, and Culture.

- The SIRVU formula concerns itself with fostering a *climate* conducive to trust.

- The HI-TRUST formula centers on the *character* and *conduct* that are crucial to trust.

- And together they generate a dynamic *culture* of trust that is resilient and replete with peak performance potential.

Since your people control the vote on whether you will be trusted or not, the SIRVU and HI-TRUST formulas aim at making it easy for them to cast their vote in your favor.

15

The SIRVU Formula

The elements of the SIRVU formula – feeling safe, informed, respected, valued, and understood – correspond to what we need to experience in order to be comfortable within any circle of people. They are the measures that we use to determine whether we are in a friendly place or not.

When settings are uncomfortable or unfriendly, trust is unlikely to thrive. Wikipedia, the collaborative on-line encyclopedia, thus defines trust as "the belief by one person that another's motivations toward them are benevolent and honest." This is precisely the type of atmosphere that the SIRVU formula seeks to engender.

Leaders with limited emotional intelligence (EQ) face an uphill battle in building a culture of trust, if they recognize the importance of trust at all. Because they are minimally attuned to their own emotions and to the emotional fields around them, they may not recognize signs that people no longer feel safe, informed, respected, valued, or understood.

They may be equally oblivious to ways in which their own attitudes and behavior have compounded the problem. Leaders with low EQ are notorious for plowing so many toxins into the cultural soil that trust cannot flourish.

But other leaders, including many who are often effective, can also miss signs of trust on the wane. This happens because distrust is clever at disguise. It can be so well hidden that it goes unnoticed by managers who are otherwise quite astute.

I saw this a few years back when a talented professional partnership asked me to help them with internal communication problems. As we met to discuss a possible engagement, I kept sensing subtle but notable misgivings, not about me, but about one another.

So I asked straight out, "Are there problems with trust within your partnership?" To a person (and virtually in unison) they said, "No." They even offered lengthy anecdotes to show how much they trusted each other.

Distrust loves to do its work quietly, unnoticed. It's a master of staying in the shadows.

But once I began the engagement, private conversations took a different turn. One by one the partners came to me saying, "Ever since you asked about trust, I've been thinking about your question. That has led me to see signs of distrust that I never noticed before." (Sometimes just asking the question, "Is trust in good repair around here?" opens our eyes to indicators of distrust that we've overlooked.)

In short order each of the partners offered specific examples of distrust within the partnership or between themselves and the staff. Within days the primary focus of my engagement shifted from improving communication to building deeper trust.

Now, these were bright, successful professionals. How could they have missed such glaring problems of distrust in their own midst? The answer is simple. Distrust loves to do its work quietly, unnoticed. It's a master of staying in the shadows. It rarely shows its hand openly, rarely draws attention to itself.

Instead it does its work surreptitiously through surrogates such as:

- compromised integrity, even if it only entails "little things"

- a pattern of broken promises and missed deadlines
- closed, self-protecting communication
- determined resistance to change
- turf-guarding
- large servings of sarcasm in comments about management
- demoralizing issues that no one dares mention
- disconnects between espoused values and actual practices
- indifference toward improving quality or performance
- unresolved resentment and frustration
- an atmosphere of disrespect or biting humor
- workplace fear, insecurity, and anxiety
- constant finger-pointing and blaming
- feelings of intimidation and powerlessness
- we-versus-them mindsets
- hesitancy to question assumptions, commitments, or time-tables
- deep suspicion of management intentions
- misgivings about how much employees are valued or respected

When I find these kinds of patterns, I know that distrust lurks somewhere in the background, fomenting discontent. If we ignore the problem, it only grows worse, for distrust never dissipates of its own accord.

The SIRVU formula aims at depriving distrust of patterns like the ones just listed. Behind each of these patterns one or more "trust-busters" are at work, and the SIRVU formula confronts their trust-busting damage head-on.

I'm obviously departing from the historic meaning of "trust-buster," which dates to the era of Teddy Roosevelt and the effort to break up powerful business trusts which dominated corporate America. The trust-busters I have in mind are actions, attitudes, or apprehensions that trigger such powerful negative emotions that any one of them, acting alone, can disrupt the emotional energy field that empowers a culture of trust.

Some of the more potent trust-busters include

- fear
- anxiety
- betrayal
- abusiveness
- blatant injustice
- character assassination
- disrespect
- cutting or demeaning remarks
- fraud
- duplicity
- deception
- dishonesty
- incompetence
- self-serving agendas

The SIRVU formula, implemented throughout your organization, serves two ends.

- First, it eliminates high-voltage trust-busters like fear, anxiety, abusiveness, betrayal, and character assassination.

- Second, it furthers a resilient climate that is able to withstand the blows that may be delivered by lower-voltage trust-busters (e.g., lackluster performance) and bounce back effectively from their effects.

We turn next, therefore, to a detailed description of each element in the SIRVU formula.

16

The SIRVU Formula:
Feeling Safe

I t's altogether proper for the SIRVU formula to begin with the word "safe," because to create a culture of trust, people must feel safe, above all else. Physically safe, naturally. But also emotionally and psychologically safe.

This means safety from threats, humiliation, intimidation, and retaliation. While relatively few work environments today present serious hazards to physical safety, they are all vulnerable to actions and attitudes that leave people feeling emotionally or psychologically unsafe.

If people do not feel safe, no other exercise in trust-building will yield telling results. As Abraham Maslow pointed out in his oft-cited hierarchy of motivational drives, the need for safety is wired into our very nature as human beings.

In infancy, long before we are able to verbalize questions, we are busy checking out the world that we have entered, trying to determine if it's a safe place. We want to know if it can be trusted. Will it come to my aid when I'm hungry? When I'm hurting? When I'm upset?

The prominence of this trust issue in early childhood explains why abuse at such a tender age yields lifelong damage. Childhood mistreatment and abuse leave the victims with gnawing questions about the world's trustworthiness, making for a lifetime of deep-seated insecurity.

Because the question of safety is so fundamental from birth, we never outgrow the need to feel safe. And at an emotional level trust and safety are so inseparably linked that they mutually reinforce each other: we feel safe with those we trust and we trust people who help us feel safe.

The presence of fear always points to a deficit of trust.

One of my most uneasy life moments came when boarding my first flight from Moscow to Siberia. As soon as I entered the passenger cabin, I noticed seats that were broken, seat belts that were inoperative, and lights that were burned out. The first question that came to mind was, "If they are this careless about internal maintenance, how careful have they been in maintaining the engines and hydraulics?"

Now, which vanished first in that moment of conjecture – my trust or my sense of safety? In essence they faded simultaneously.

For this reason, the most powerful trust-busters are those associated with feeling unsafe. Fear, of course, heads the list. To the degree that fear is present, trust is constricted, or even choked out altogether. A famous question from Jesus highlights the incompatibility of fear and trust. The Gospels quote him as asking his fearful followers, "Why are you afraid, you men of little faith?"

While "faith" and "trust" are different words in English, they are identical in the original language of the Gospels. At a conceptual level we retain this identity in modern speech, where the statements "I trust you" and "I have faith in you" are fundamentally synonymous. So Jesus was saying in effect, "The presence of fear points to a deficit of trust."

Anxiety, a close cousin of fear, is another trust-buster. It, too, connotes a sense of being unsafe. While fear usually centers on a specific, identifiable threat, the threat in anxiety is typically more vague. It's often little more than a looming apprehension that some possible future development could prove undesirable, unpleasant, or even unbearable.

Because the anticipated threat is so lacking in detail, anxiety leaves us perplexed about how to respond, uncertain about which course to take. The Greeks captured this perplexity in their word for anxiety, which literally means "to be of two minds."

High levels of trust and elevated states of fear do not co-exist.

Interestingly, in the Sermon on the Mount Jesus also asks, "Why are you so anxious, you men of little faith?" As with fear, acute anxiety is evidence of diminished trust. A pilot who trusts his aircraft doesn't become anxious just because he encounters turbulence. Nor does a woman who trusts her husband live in constant anxiety about him being unfaithful.

From a diagnostic standpoint, widespread fear and anxiety within organizations are clear indicators that trust is in short supply. People are reluctant, however, to talk openly about their fears (and to a lesser extent their anxieties), especially in work settings and among fellow workers. Men in particular want to avoid seeming weak in the eyes of peers, which is a risk they take if they acknowledge fear or anxiety.

In addition, an interesting paradox is at work here. If trust is high enough for people to freely admit their fears and discuss them openly, the very strength of that trust indicates that there are likely few job-related fears to discuss. High levels of trust and elevated states of fear do not co-exist.

By the same token, once fear becomes a serious morale or trust factor, people are already intimidated. They no longer feel safe enough to speak "on the record" about why they feel unsafe.

Thus an unwilling conspiracy of silence develops around the subject of specific behaviors, policies, groups, or individuals that are sparking fear. If workers speak of their fears and anxieties at all, it's in muttered remarks, whispered to one another in guarded, hushed tones. Or they make quiet head nods to new employees to warn, "Watch out for that person over there." (Hence the joke in HR circles that what new hires want most from an orientation session are the three B's: when are the breaks, where are the bathrooms, and who are the people to beware of.)

People are more likely to be forthright about their workplace fears and anxieties in conversations with outsiders, where they feel free of peer pressure and have no concern about retaliation. This is why consultants or anonymous surveys frequently uncover deeper patterns of fear, anxiety, and distrust than management itself perceives.

This is not an indictment of management. It's simply an acknowledgment that fear and anxiety are not always easily detected. To borrow a noted phrase from submarine warfare, these two trust-busters – fear and anxiety – prefer to "run silent, run deep."

But observant leaders can use telltale signs to recognize that fear and anxiety are at work, even when they are otherwise hidden from sight. Some of the more frequent indicators of a fearful or anxious culture are:

- hesitancy to take personal initiative

- widespread defensiveness

- reluctance to challenge the viewpoint of managers or of strong opinion leaders within the group

- unwillingness to acknowledge personal responsibility for an error in judgment or some lapse in performance
- unwritten codes that "we don't talk about that around here"
- nervous concern about communicating bad news to superiors
- disproportionately small numbers of people willing to consider positions as supervisors or managers
- a prevailing attitude that "play it safe" and "keep your head down" are the primary rules of the road
- waiting for an unequivocal sign-off from management before chancing any action
- undue preoccupation with obtaining leadership's assurance that a job is being done well
- insistence on detailed document trails to show that every action was properly approved
- a tendency for people to become disproportionately upset or fretful when something goes wrong

---

When fear grips us, we feel an urge to shrink back from the threat, or even to run from it. With anxiety we are torn, unsure what action to take. Neither fear nor anxiety, then, moves us forward decisively.

This is why organizations that seek peak performance must marginalize fear and anxiety. These emotions are like a virus in any organization, spreading a contagion of mistrust far and wide.

As long as human societies have existed, this virus has waged war on trust. But in today's world of business, the battle is being fought on more fronts than ever, in no small part because of the unprecedented pace of competition and innovation. Both competition and innovation demand constant change. And with change there is always a certain degree of uncertainty, the ideal breeding ground for fear and anxiety.

Change also entails trade-offs. In these trade-offs some elements of the organization inevitably gain strength at the expense of others. Resources, and often budgets, are likewise reapportioned.

While management sees these shifts as tactical necessities or (in the case of more sweeping change) essential strategic realignments, workers view them differently. Workers have a propensity to interpret change through the lens of winning or losing personally. Was my project a winner or loser in this change? How did our department do – did we come out on top or toward the bottom? Am I in a more advantageous position as a result of the latest restructure of our department? Or am I now in a disadvantaged position?

These questions preoccupy workers because employees typically view "losing" as a potential threat to job security, increased pay, and promotability. As a consequence, the mere rumor of restructure, budget cuts, downsizing, mergers, or plummeting stock prices can be enough to usher in fear and anxiety.

The process usually proceeds along these lines. The rumor of wholesale change starts people speculating about whether they will end up winners or losers after all is said and done. Those who see themselves as potential losers then grow anxious about what awaits. And as the number of self-perceived "losers" multiplies, anxiety within the entire organization grows accordingly, sometimes geometrically.

Here again is a paradox. Restructuring, "right-sizing," acquisitions, and mergers (whether we're speaking of departments, divisions, or entire companies) hold the promise of increased returns for stockholders and the opportunity for upper managers to earn handsome bonuses through improved efficiency. For these two groups reorganizing is loaded with potential wins.

By contrast, among workers and lower tiers of management only some will be winners. The rest will be "losers" in the competition for prestige, prominence, promotions, and pay, or even retention. They greet the change with trepidation, not excitement.

So long as fear and anxiety remain relatively mild, the impact on productivity and trust may be limited. But as the rumors gain credence, an elaborate political dance begins. On the theory that the name of the game is now "survival of the best connected," people start trying to position themselves to avoid being a "loser" in the ultimate outcome.

Anyone seen as a contender for any of their resources is no longer viewed as a colleague or collaborator, but a competitor. Rivalry supplants cooperation. Friends become adversaries. Turf-protecting becomes more determined. In this atmosphere trust has a hard time holding on. And often it doesn't.

As these kinds of scenarios unfold, odds increase that the level of anxiety or fear will damage trust so thoroughly that the anticipated productivity gains from the new alignment are never realized. Even if people who perceive themselves as potential losers eventually find their worst fears unfounded, weeks or months of fear and anxiety will leave trust bruised and bleeding.

This, then, is why leaders should guard against frequent reorganizations or a steady pace of non-essential change. When change is persistent, anxieties from one change never have time to settle before announcement of another change adds further anxiety to the mix. And in the case of sweeping or transformational change, anxiety takes significant time to subside. This may be why studies find notably lower levels of trust in organizations that have been through mergers or acquisitions within the previous two years.

Trust-formation must precede transformation.

Trust-Centered Leadership™ thus presumes that change – especially wholesale change – will inflict a blow on trust, and it takes proactive measures to minimize the injury. The best proactive measure is to optimize trust during periods of relative stability so that when change does come, the reservoir of trust is well supplied.

Deep trust, built up in advance, provides two essential defenses when unsettling events arise.

- First, it gives the organization greater resistance to fear and anxiety whenever they seek a foothold.

- Second, it lessens the ability of fear and anxiety to drain trust entirely before these two trust-busters are defeated and turned back.

This simple observation thus leads to another cornerstone principle in Trust-Centered Leadership™: trust-formation must precede transformation. Trust-building is a vital enterprise even in organizations where trust is currently in good repair, because wholesale change can be thrust upon them unexpectedly and at any moment. When this happens, every organization needs the deepest reservoir of trust possible.

17

Countering the Threat of Fear

T hus far, as we have examined lethal trust-busters, we have treated fear and anxiety as almost a single entity. They do, indeed, work masterfully together, mutually reinforcing one another. Yet I've dealt with a number of anxiety-ridden situations where no significant fear was present.

It's helpful, therefore, to think of these two as collaborative trust-busters, but separate threats. And because they are differing realities, we need distinct strategies for dealing with each one. This chapter focuses on counteracting fear in the workplace. Chapter 18 looks at antidotes to anxiety.

To see where your organization is susceptible to fear, simply ask, "What goes on around here that could leave people feeling threatened?" Your list might include such things as:

- backbiting and back-stabbing
- heavy-handed supervision and discipline
- angry outbursts, whether from managers or peers
- intimidation and ultimatums
- abusive language and name calling
- degrading remarks
- verbal attacks
- bullying

- hostile gestures or posture
- derisive nick-names
- retaliation, perceived or real
- belittling or humiliating remarks
- finger-pointing and fault-finding
- unrealistic or unmanageable deadlines
- racist or sexist humor

Leaders committed to Trust-Centered Leadership™ not only avoid this kind of conduct themselves, they do not tolerate it within their organization. They see to it that standards of conduct are spelled out clearly. Then they hold themselves and everyone else accountable to these standards.

To this end, at the very outset of new leadership roles, we must state our commitment to an atmosphere in which every worker feels physically and emotionally safe, as well as informed, respected, valued, and understood.

Then, no more than a few weeks later, we should initiate a process to make appropriate revisions to existing standards (or to develop formal standards where none have previously existed) to foster a culture of trust. These standards need to emerge from group dialogue if at all possible, not from a unilateral pronouncement on our part.

There are at least six reasons for making this a group exercise rather than an initiative where a manager puts the guidelines together with minimal input from others.

- First, people are far more likely to take standards seriously when they have a direct role in setting them.

- Second, the process itself causes people to start thinking reflectively – perhaps for the first time ever – about what it means to act in such a way that their actions create a trust-friendly atmosphere.

- Third, the collective wisdom of the group usually identifies specific threats felt within the organization that a leader who is new to the organization might not sense.

- Fourth, groups like this usually set more exacting standards for themselves than we might have the confidence to promulgate as a new manager.

- Fifth, if we as leaders are unknowingly doing things that hinder a culture of trust, group dialogue may bring that to the fore to help us become aware of it.

- Sixth, because these standards are developed by the group, they more readily become part of the organization's culture and retain their "shelf life" long after we have moved to duties elsewhere.

The dialogue that drives this process should provide specific and extensive input from stakeholders in the organization. Where our organization is a small work group or task force, it may be feasible for every stakeholder to participate directly. In larger organizations the work is better accomplished through stakeholder representatives.

Whatever the format, we want to pose two questions to frame the dialogue.

- First, what standards of conduct should we set for ourselves so that everyone in our organization feels safe and unthreatened, both physically and emotionally, in our workplace?

- And second, what standards should we set for ourselves so that we always treat one another with dignity and respect? (Respect, you will recall, is the second element of the SIRVU formula.)

These two questions are best treated separately, but always with the other held in view.

The reason for addressing both of these questions is that genuine mutual respect puts a check on most threatening and abusive behavior. Indeed, a secondary meaning of respect is "to avoid harming or interfering with," as when we speak of respecting someone's privacy.

Yet, we should not frame the dialogue about standards as simply a discussion of respect. We need to raise the explicit issue of helping people feel safe, and we should raise it first. Why?

The answer is, we want people fully engaged in this dialogue, participating fully from the very beginning. And the issue of feeling personally safe is likely to engage people more fully and more quickly than a dialogue about respect.

Moreover, if the dialogue is framed primarily or exclusively around creating respect, the urgency of making people feel safe – the first and foremost requirement for a culture of trust – can easily be lost, not only on the participants in the dialogue, but eventually to the entire organization.

It has also been my experience that people who are prone to bullying or threatening behavior won't be held in check by simple reminders that they are expected to treat people with respect. They will retort, "Oh, I respect them," then continue unabated in their inappropriate behavior.

The standards must therefore be straightforward and specific in marking fear-inducing behavior as inappropriate. And this will only happen if the question of making people feel safe is a prominent part of the dialogue.

As the leader, even though we are only facilitating the development of standards, not setting them ourselves, we may need to "nudge" the process from time to time so that it does not overlook or ignore any type of threatening conduct. The categories listed toward the top of this chapter could serve as an initial checklist (but by no means an exhaustive one) of behaviors that the final standards should target.

There is one proviso, however. While the desired outcome of this exercise is a workplace where people feel safe and unthreatened, the goal is not absolute freedom from anything that carries a threat. Otherwise motivation and discipline would have only carrots, never a stick at their disposal.

Were we to outlaw everything that makes people feel threatened, we would rob ourselves of the very tools we may need to serve notice on workers who persist in trust-busting behavior. Of necessity, then, the final standards must preserve the freedom for management to issue warnings and penalties for poor performance or infractions of standards.

On the other hand, it is altogether appropriate for the standards to address the question of the "tone" that should surround disciplinary action. Aggressive, demeaning, bullying behavior cannot be justified simply because it occurs in the context of correcting underperformance or misconduct.

Once standards of conduct are in place, our work as leaders has only begun. It's now our duty to see that everyone complies with the standards and that serious infractions are immediately and unfailingly confronted.

Tackling these infractions, especially at first when violations may be commonplace, can be a delicate balancing act for the leader who seeks to maximize trust. On one hand, people not only need to see the leader emphasizing standards of trust-friendly conduct and modeling them personally, they also need to know that their leader calls people to task who violate these boundaries. On the other hand, calling someone's hand publicly risks alienating that person (and his or her friends) and adding to distrust.

A more artful approach is to correct privately (either personally or through the appropriate front-line supervisor), at the same time making everyone aware that non-compliance with the standards is not being condoned.

For example, we will inevitably need to restate the standards of conduct periodically, if for no other reason than to keep them fresh in people's minds. These restatements are a perfect time to say, almost in an off-hand remark, "I believe you know by now that these standards of conduct are important to me and to all of us. And the few times I've seen them violated in our organization, we've addressed the matter privately with the party involved. Out of these conversations I believe we now have greater compliance with our standards."

We must have a zero tolerance for conduct that contributes to an atmosphere of fear, intimidation, or abuse.

All of this may seem like a lot of work, first to develop standards of conduct, then to communicate them regularly, and finally to deal personally with infractions. But remember, we are working to disarm fear, the worst trust-buster of the lot. Even if we are less than consistent in disciplining violations of other standards, we must have a zero tolerance for conduct that contributes to an atmosphere of fear, intimidation, or abuse.

18

The SIRVU Formula: Feeling Informed

Like fear, anxiety in the workplace tends to diminish the feeling of safety and security. But anxiety is less a response to threatening behavior or an imminent danger than to a sense of an uncertain, precarious future. The key word here is "precarious." We don't become anxious simply because the future is uncertain, for everyone knows that the future is always uncertain.

No, anxiety is tied to some possible future development which we view with apprehension and uneasiness. It's somewhat like sailing into uncharted waters, the kind that ancient map makers annotated with the words, "Sea monsters lurk here." Anxiety approaches the uncharted water with foreboding premonitions that things may not work out well.

Because so many unknowns can trigger anxiety, most having nothing to do with the workplace, it's unrealistic to envision a workforce in which every employee is anxiety free. No leader could accomplish such a feat. What leaders can do, however, is to minimize the number of anxiety-provoking events that transpire within their organization.

And what are those events? In a business context they are basically things which raise uncertainty or doubts about what we might call an employee's personal vested interests, such as continued employment, the profile of the job, working relationships, pay, promotion, project evaluations, performance reviews, visibility to upper management, or access to decision-making.

And the pivotal terms in this statement are "doubt" and "uncertainty." They are the culprits. Actions, changes, and policies that raise neither uncertainty nor doubt are unlikely to elevate anxiety.

Uncertainty and/or doubt generally result from lack of critical information. The missing information is easily identified with the question, "What more would you need to know in order to resolve this uncertainty, this doubt?"

Which leads to the second element of the SIRVU formula – people need to feel informed. In the absence of information people will still persist in trying to determine the meaning of things which they experience, observe, or become aware of. And when information is unavailable to them, they will assign meaning by resorting to the only other mechanism at their disposal – speculation.

Speculation itself would not be particularly dangerous, were it not for its tendency to arouse suspicion. Have you ever noticed that when people speculate, they never seem to presume that something good is afoot? Speculation never says, "You know, the executive team has been in lengthy meetings every morning for the last four days. I bet something really wonderful is about to happen!!"

Instead, speculation seems inexorably biased toward believing that the worst is going on or that people are up to no good. That's why speculation leads so frequently to suspicion and a questioning of intentions. From suspicion and questioned intentions it's a short path to distrust. The process frequently runs along these lines:

- Uncertainty fuels speculation
- Speculation sparks suspicion
- Suspicion multiplies the number of perceived dangers
- The number of perceived dangers triggers anxiety
- Anxiety engenders fear

- Fear and anxiety choke out trust

Trust-Centered Leadership™ never sits idly by and allows this cycle of speculation, suspicion, and fear to go unchecked. Instead, Trust-Centered Leadership™ disrupts the cycle by excelling at the age-old adage: communicate, communicate, communicate.

The purpose of copious communication is not merely to keep work flowing smoothly and to make decision-making timely and well-informed. It also has the purpose, equally urgent, of disarming the kind of speculation that produces anxiety.

Most people are unlikely to invest trust in those who treat them with disrespect.

Communication also lessens the likelihood of people feeling "left in the dark," which never enhances trust. I find it intriguing, indeed, that the phrase "left in the dark" has become synonymous with being uninformed. Anyone who has experienced pitch blackness, perhaps in an unfamiliar spot, knows the feeling of apprehension that begins to build if the experience becomes prolonged.

Something similar happens inside of us when we feel "left in the dark" about plans, considerations, or emerging developments that carry significant potential impact on our work and our lives.

Being left in the dark is also a frequent complaint of those who feel as though they are either not respected or not valued, two other elements of the SIRVU formula. Most people are unlikely to invest trust in those who treat them with disrespect or who leave the impression that they are not personally valued. Being "left in the dark" thus threatens trust on multiple fronts.

Because good leaders are usually adept at facing uncertainty without becoming unsettled, they can easily miss the fact that many of their people are cut from a different piece of cloth. Uncertainty disturbs many people quite deeply.

And the tendency to overlook this difference becomes more pronounced the higher we go in leadership. Those who succeed to senior levels of leadership are typically people who have demonstrated an ability to function effectively in the midst of significant ambiguity.

This ability to cope with ambiguity may be natural to them, or they may have learned it along the way. In either event, it is easy for them to forget that many who look to them for leadership do not manage well with prolonged ambiguity.

To keep anxiety at bay, leaders must keep uncertainties from multiplying in the minds of their people. When rumors are afoot, give people clarifying information as quickly as possible. When major changes are made, err on the side of giving people more information than they want rather than on the side of giving them too little information. Help them feel informed.

Here again it's essential for leaders to assume the perceptual position of the people they lead, as we emphasized in chapter thirteen. One admiral I worked for was particularly sensitive to this need. I was the most junior officer on his staff, having been commissioned only three years before after a ten-year enlisted career.

Whenever the staff was considering pivotal changes in policy, at some point the admiral would invariably turn to me and ask, "Mike, what will this decision look like and feel like to sailors in the enlisted ranks?" This was his way of maintaining the perceptual position of those he led.

Whatever your own technique, maintain the discipline of looking at change through the eyes of your people. From their perspective determine what you need to communicate and how you need to communicate it to keep anxiety in check. Remember, trust-busters like fear and anxiety are always waiting in the wings, ready to rush on stage if you will simply give them an opportunity.

19

The SIRVU Formula:
Feeling Respected and Valued

O nce people feel safe and informed, they next need to feel respected, valued, and understood, the last three elements of the SIRVU formula. Respect has a variety of connotations. "To respect someone" may mean we admire that person. Or it can carry the sense of holding the person's views and wisdom in high regard, e.g., "I respect Joe, and he says we should make this investment."

In terms of creating a culture of trust, however, we use the word respect primarily in the sense of 1) treating people with courtesy and 2) safe-guarding their dignity. Worded negatively, respect means we are neither rude nor thoughtless in the way we act toward people. We do not speak of them derisively. We never purposefully embarrass them, belittle them, or humiliate them. We never respond to them dismissively. And we do these things behind their backs no more than we do them to their face.

Being treated with respect is key to feeling that we are valued. When people treat us disrespectfully, it's hard to believe that we are important to them. And since we do not typically trust people who leave us feeling unimportant, trust is unlikely to be deeply rooted in a culture where disrespect is commonplace.

Respect in the workplace suffers from deteriorating standards of respect in our society. It begins with children who are allowed to speak to parents and other authority figures in disrespectful tones that were unthinkable two generations ago. Training in common courtesies and proper etiquette, both of which aim at thoughtful, civil treatment of others, has steadily declined for decades.

Another contributor has been what passes as humor in entertainment. With the advent of television sitcoms like *All in the Family* and *The Jeffersons* television began churning out comedy shows in which "being funny" meant showing yourself more creative than anyone else in the way you insulted people or put them down. Two generations of young people have now grown up thinking that disrespect is a laughing matter and that it's okay to laugh when people are on the receiving end of even the most hurtful insults.

Some of the more common discourtesies and disrespectful attitudes we see in the workplace include:

- side bar conversations around the conference table when someone else is making a presentation or offering an extended observation

- failure to answer emails, voice mails, and other communications in an appropriate time frame, or at least to acknowledge the communiqué with a response to the sender indicating that a fuller reply must be delayed for whatever reason

- being routinely late for meetings and conferences

- derisive nicknames for unpopular fellow workers

- circulating rumors that besmirch or discredit someone

- mean-spirited practical jokes

- failure to say "please" and "thank you" as a matter of routine

- not giving people adequate advance notice that promised deadlines will be missed

Issues of respect, however, go far beyond simple courtesies. And as the leader, you must model the type of mutual respect you expect among those you lead.

For example, in most larger organizations I have led there has been the occasional odd-duck, someone who did not quite fit the social or personality mold of others in the group. Commonly these odd ducks are shown minimal respect. People make fun of them outside of their hearing, or sometimes even in their presence. Peers snicker beneath their breath when the odd duck offers a comment during a meeting. Or fellow workers studiously avoid sitting or socializing with the odd duck at company events.

When I recognize this pattern at work, I make it my duty as a leader to become the odd duck's champion. I go out of my way to be seen visiting with odd ducks in the hallway. I seek them out at social events, where others are likely to take note of the people with whom the boss visits. When someone makes a derisive comment about them in my presence, I move immediately to counter by pointing out the importance of what they contribute to our effort.

And when odd ducks speak up in group meetings, I purposefully do two things. I pay them rapt, undivided attention to convey to everyone else that I consider this person a valued member of our team. And I creatively find a way to tie something in the odd duck's remarks – even if their remarks are not directly on subject – to a critical point under consideration. (I'm a firm believer that with a little imagination you can link any subject to any other subject.)

When there is no immediate and apparent link between the odd duck's comment and our immediate purposes, I am known to create a link by saying, "You know, your comment reminds me of a story that happened . . ." And then I relate an event in which I make an obvious tie to something they have said. But I also design the story so that I can tie specific elements in the story to the discussion at hand.

You may question why I should go to such effort to affirm the odd duck. The answer is two-fold. First, to convince people that everyone is deserving of respect in our organization, I must model it convincingly myself.

But there is a second and perhaps even more important objective. After a while, if people become convinced that I will protect the dignity and the self-worth of even the odd ducks, they feel assured that I will protect their own dignity, as well. This awareness then creates a tremendous sense of safety that everyone cherishes within the organization and which adds to the level of trust.

Feeling valued and feeling respected are closely related, but with significant distinctions. We can be indifferent to people, yet still respect them. (For instance, when standing in line at a checkout counter I treat others in line with respect, even though I may never see them again in my life.) But I can never be indifferent about a person or object that I value.

As a consequence, when people feel valued they translate this to mean that leaders or peers care for them in a way that respect alone will not convey. When we feel that someone truly cares for us, it diminishes any anxiety about that person doing us harm. Feeling valued thus adds to the sense of safety.

In most organizations the most common tool for helping people feel valued is recognition. Recognition can take many forms. Recognition events within the organization are always important. But periodic recognition events, whether monthly, quarterly, or annually, can sometimes lead to considerable lag time between the laudable performance and the actual recognition of it.

Recognition is far more effective when this lag time is kept to a minimum. Whenever people do well, they need to know immediately that leadership recognizes and applauds their performance. Added recognition may come later in some public venue, at some special event. But immediate recognition through a phone call, email, personal comment, or note is vital to making people feel valued.

Of special note is the research we have already cited from Terry Bacon. His survey of over 500 workers revealed that "women and people in their twenties have significantly greater needs for reward and recognition from their manager and for feeling that their manager values them."[46]

It also pays great dividends for leaders to be overt and unapologetic about telling people individually, one-on-one, how much they are valued. Avery Johnson, who in his first full year as an NBA coach was named coach of the year, describes his success by saying that he first makes sure that his players know how much he cares for them and their families. Then, and only then, does he get down to the matter of plays, practice, and discipline.

He even has specific ways of demonstrating how much he cares for the players and their families. He is known for having children of players spend a night at his house. When the team is on the road and in a city where one of the players has children, he is known to allow the player to miss practice to have some time with his kids.

Even though Avery is referred to as "the little general" because of his tough discipline and work ethic, his players do not resent the demands he places on them on the court because they know how much he cares for them off the court. They feel genuinely valued.

We communicate how much people are valued in many day-to-day behaviors that fall short of inviting their children for a sleepover. None of these day-to-day behaviors is more powerful than simply giving people undivided attention. In today's hectic world, the most valuable thing most people have is their time. When a

---

[46] Terry Bacon, *What People Want*, p. 46.

leader grants us a claim on his or her time and attention, we invariably feel affirmed and valued.

The key, however, is for the leader to give people attention that is genuinely undivided. I've seen managers advertise an open door policy, but people who step through the open door must carry on a conversation while the leader scans emails. Or listens with one ear while thumbing through a report. Or checks a Blackberry every time it vibrates.

When a leader is grants us a claim on his or her time and attention, we invariably feel affirmed and valued.

Practiced this way, an open door policy may result in workers feeling more freedom to approach the leader. But it does nothing to make a worker feel valued. In fact, such behavior has just the opposite effect. The impression left on workers is, "I'm not as valuable to the boss as the reports on his desk."

Whenever I've been in roles where I simply was overwhelmed with pressing reports, inquiries, or research that demanded my attention, I've developed a qualified open door policy. I've stated unequivocally, "I need to protect my schedule from 7:00 to 10:00 each morning to get the things cleared off of my desk that I'm obligated to take care of. If you would do me the favor of foregoing phone calls or drop-in visits until after that time, you will put me in a better position to give you undistracted attention when you need to talk to me."

Rarely does an employee or peer have a problem that is so urgent that it simply cannot wait until 10:00 a.m. And when exceptional situations do arise, I'm certainly willing to set the rule aside. But the rule itself says to my people, "You are valuable to me, and I want to able to affirm that value with the quality of attention I give you when you need my time."

20

The SIRVU Formula: Feeling Understood

U ndivided attention also goes a long way in satisfying the fifth element of the SIRVU formula, feeling understood. No nation in history has had the benefit of a workforce as educated as ours. People are well informed. And they know they are well informed.

They therefore believe that their opinion counts for something. They likewise feel that they have enough to offer that their views, concerns, and preferences deserve a fair hearing.

If we do not value our people's insights, opinions, and concerns, our indifference easily translates into a conclusion on their part that we are likewise indifferent toward them personally. In a word, that we do not value them. Helping people feel understood is therefore crucial in helping them feel valued, which in turn is vital for building trust.

This is not to say that people expect us to implement every tidbit of wisdom and counsel they offer us. People will accept a decision that goes against their preferences if they feel that in the process of reaching the decision, the leader took their concerns and viewpoints into consideration.

Nor is it necessary (or even wise) for leaders to rush out and take an opinion poll of their people every time a decision is in the balance. Rather, what is called for is an atmosphere in which leaders seem approachable and in which people can gain the ear of their leaders with relative ease.

The precise input mechanism may be an open door policy, email, town hall meetings, web surveys, focus groups, an on-line suggestion box, or any of another dozen possible communication instruments. Ideally, in fact, it should involve as many venues as practical.

The goal is to create a prevailing sense, based on reality, that people have a simple means of voicing their concerns or making input into decisions that affect them. Not only this, people need to feel that their input will be cordially received and thoughtfully considered.

In his autobiography General Colin Powell tells how, as a base commander, he had a chauffer and a command car always at his beckoning. But he chose to walk from the office to his home each afternoon, telling people that it was a good opportunity to get some exercise. The exercise was of course beneficial.

But his greater purpose was to be seen making his way home each day at a predictable time, taking routes that gave everyone easy access to him. Anyone could stop him and converse. There were no gatekeepers, no security cordons. And many, including enlisted men of every rank, became comfortable convening a sidewalk conversation with their commander. These impromptu discussions, he notes, provided him knowledge of serious concerns that he could have discovered in no other way.

When Admiral Elmo Zumwalt was Chief of Naval Operations, one of his modes of making himself accessible was to drop in unannounced on a Navy base and put out the word that he would be in the cafeteria having coffee, should anyone want to come by and talk.

I remember his visit to my own duty station. He was sitting at a table enjoying his coffee, surrounded at any given time by dozens of officers and enlisted personnel who were firing questions at him on every conceivable subject.

At the time Admiral Zumwalt was making changes to uniform and grooming standards, and his initiatives were unpopular with the "old salts," who felt that he was tossing too much tradition to the winds. Some of these critics were represented in the ensemble around his table, and they did not hesitate to voice their disagreement with his policies. He took in their reservations graciously, explained his reasons for pursuing the course he had chosen, and sprinkled his comments with disarming humor.

I don't think he changed anyone's mind. Months later the people who disagreed with him were still vocal in criticizing his initiatives. But they had a newfound respect for him, because he had gone so far out of his way to listen.

As leaders who want our people to feel understood, it's *how* we listen that is as important as the listening itself. There are several little "tricks of the trade" that are simple to practice, but which make a vital difference in helping people feel that their leader has truly listened.

- **Be singularly attentive.** This is an extension of giving people undivided attention, which we discussed above. Engage the other party fully with your eyes, your posture, and your body language.

  If a conversation begins at an inconvenient moment because other things demand immediate attention, or if a conversation goes longer than anticipated and impinges on time you must protect for something else, either wrap up the discussion politely or set a time to continue it. "Susan, I appreciate talking to you about this issue and we obviously have more to discuss. Right now, however, I have an item that demands my attention. Could we set a time to continue this conversation when I won't have something distracting me?"

Don't leave it as, "Let me get back to you." Set a time to continue. Then follow through. If a conflict develops with the time you've agreed to, reschedule. But avoid rescheduling repeatedly. Otherwise you risk leaving the impression that the continuation of the conversation is actually not so important to you after all. Everything else on your schedule seems to take priority over it.

- **Ask several follow-on questions.** Questions are the way we invite others to extend a conversation. And nothing conveys the sense that we are genuinely listening more effectively than for us to extend this invitation several times in the course of a discussion. Make it a point to ask follow-on questions, two or three as a minimum, even more in a protracted conversation.

The questions can be very simple, very straightforward. Here are some I use with regularity:

- "I want to be sure I understand what you mean when you use the term X. Could you elaborate just a bit on what that phrase means to you?"

- "Can you give me a few more details about X?"

- "Can you give me another example of what you're talking about?"

- "What problems do you foresee if we take this course of action?"

- "Have you seen this done anywhere else?"

The list could obviously go on and on. The precise questions themselves are less important than taking time to pose them. The mere fact that you asked questions helps people feel that they were heard.

- **Lean into the conversation.** Posture sends a tell-tale signal about how much or how little a given discussion interests us. When we are no longer engaged by a conversation, we start looking around, fiddling with something in our hands, turning away slightly, or even stepping back from the conversation to put greater distance between us and the speaker.

On the other hand, notice what happens when people seated at a table get into an enthralling exchange. They lean forward and look intently at the other party.

The more frequently you "lean into a conversation" the more the other person will sense your true interest. We're not referring here necessarily to leaning your body forward literally. Unless you are seated at a desk or table, this would seem awkward and unnatural, both to you and to the other party (although you should take advantage of situations where you are seated and have this option).

But just mentally picturing yourself seated and leaning forward to engage the conversation will have a telling and positive impact on your posture, the warmth of your eye contact, and the tone of your voice. It will all happen unconsciously. But the other person will pick up on it at an unconscious level. And without quite knowing why, they will feel as though you are affirming your interest in their comments.

If I'm seated at a desk while talking to someone on the phone or participating in a teleconference, I literally lean forward when I want to communicate a compelling idea or raise a key question. Since we are on the phone, the other parties can't see my posture, but they can hear the difference in my tone and quality of voice. It's a simple technique, but one with tremendous payoffs.

- **Affirm people facially.** When I shadow clients for a day to watch them in action, I closely monitor the quality of facial feedback they offer others in conversation. This is important because few people have any idea of what their facial expression communicates as they listen. After all, how many of us have ever seen a video of ourselves listening intently to what someone else is saying?

For example, one of my clients prided himself at listening attentively, yet he knew that workers were hesitant to come to him with ideas or concerns. He was at a loss to explain the problem. But in our very first conversation I was able to recognize what was happening. He is a person (and there are multitudes of them) who, when listening intently, has a tight pensive scowl on his face. It's his way of concentrating.

But the expression was easily misread as strong disagreement or even anger. He had no idea he was doing it. Nevertheless, the more engaged he became in listening to his people, the more his facial features tightened, so that the feedback led the other person to question his receptivity.

One little technique can neutralize these types of unhelpful, inadvertent messages. Remind yourself while listening – and while speaking – to put an expression on your face that is akin to being very slightly amused. Just a tiny little smile on your lips will suffice. You don't want to overdo it to such an extent that the other person begins to wonder if you think his or her comments are laughable.

But just a tiny smile on your lips will actually brighten your eyes and will relax all the other muscles of the cheeks and neck. Then add an occasional slight head nod, made at the appropriate moment, as if to say, "Yes, I understand. Keep going." A friendly countenance with assuring head nods is one of the most powerful techniques for helping people feel that they are truly being heard.

- **Stay attuned to the tone of your voice.** Just as it is important to soften the expressions on our face, for many people it is also important to soften the tone of voice in conversations in which they need to be perceived as truly listening.

One of the most important things about a softer tone of voice is that it dampens any defensiveness we may otherwise communicate. This is especially true if someone is criticizing something we have done or is raising a question about the wisdom of some decision we have made.

Defensiveness is one of the greatest enemies of communication. When I'm defensive I can't listen fully to the other person. And when my defensiveness comes through in the tone of my voice, others easily conclude that I'm more inclined to protect myself or my reputation than to listen genuinely to their concerns.

Make it a point, therefore, to monitor yourself and notice the moment when feelings of defensiveness start rising within you. Move immediately to soften the tone of your voice. Interestingly, not only will this little change lessen the likelihood that you will come across to the other party as defensive, it will actually reduce your own defensive feelings, too.

The first step in helping people feel understood is to provide easy, user-friendly avenues through which people can make their input. To cement the sense of being understood, it is equally important for people to receive feedback on suggestions, ideas, or expressions of concern. Feedback is the only way for people to feel assured that they have indeed been heard.

There is no one "right way" for feedback to occur. The most important thing is that it should happen often enough and frequently enough that people know that their opinions are treated as worthwhile.

It's especially important for feedback to celebrate ideas and suggestions that are particularly insightful or beneficial. It's what some people call "validating people's contributions." One purpose for creating open, unhampered communication between people and their leaders is to give leadership the added benefit of the creativity and imagination that their people possess. The most innovative ideas in an organization can come from the most unexpected sources.

Once people recognize that their constructive recommendations are often accepted, implemented, and celebrated, with due credit given to the person who offered the suggestion, other people quickly start putting their own creativity to work in the form of noteworthy ideas.

Now, when we create such open lines of communication, we inevitably receive a certain amount of input that is either unworkable or ill-advised. People rarely see all the complexities in a situation that their leader must consider. A steady stream of impractical inputs might therefore seem a waste of the leader's time, becoming a rationale for foregoing an open communication process.

But even unworkable suggestions and input are helpful. They show leaders where people need more information to see the full picture. Or they give the leader feedback on concerns that preoccupy their people. And often, even though the suggestion itself may be impractical, it calls attention to problems that beg to be addressed.

When we look at the HI-TRUST formula, many considerations that have surfaced in our discussion of the SIRVU formula will appear once more. The two formulas are somewhat like two sides of the same coin. The SIRVU formula highlights what people have to feel in order to trust their leaders. And the HI-TRUST formula highlights what leaders must do in order to create a SIRVU environment. We therefore turn next to the seven traits that comprise the HI-TRUST formula.

21

The HI-TRUST Formula

We have repeatedly noted that trust is built primarily on patterns of behavior. This does not mean that trust results from putting on some type of act. Any effort along these lines is doomed from the outset. Sooner or later people will see through the act. And once they do, the very hypocrisy they discover will shatter trust thoroughly.

Behavior must stem from inner values, attitudes, and beliefs that serve to provide a natural footing for trust-building behavior. The HI-TRUST formula brings together both inner and outer dimensions of trust building through:

- Humility
- Integrity
- Truth
- Responsiveness
- Unblemished Fair Play
- Support and Encouragement
- Team Care

To create a High-Trust, Peak-Performance Organization these qualities must be characteristic not only of leadership, but of the organization itself.

When I make this statement to mid-level executives in very large organizations, they sometimes reply, "But even if I practice Trust-Centered Leadership™ at my level of the organization, the management above me doesn't practice what it takes to build a high-trust culture. So it sounds like Trust-Centered Leadership™ has little benefit in my situation."

I always respond to managers in situations like this by acknowledging a certain amount of truth to what they say. The impact of Trust-Centered Leadership™ will doubtlessly be more limited in a company like theirs than in scenarios where trust-building is championed from the top. Yet, to acknowledge that the benefit is limited is a far cry from saying that the benefit is minimal or nonexistent.

If you are a leader in this type of setting, you can still have a telling impact by making your own unit a Trust-Bonded Organization™.

- Once you build a High-Trust, Peak-Performance Organization, it's likely to outperform peer units in the company. As a minimum this will catch the eye of upper management and lead to inquiries about the secret of your success. At this point you have created a forum to convince management above you that Trust-Centered Leadership™ pays significant dividends.

- The success of your High-Trust, Peak-Performance Organization should normally accelerate your own advancement to more significant posts, where you can build an even larger high-trust culture and spread the concepts of Trust-Centered Leadership™ more broadly in your company.

Moreover, your present organization, limited in size though it may be, is a great test bed for you to begin mastering the skills and techniques of Trust-Centered Leadership™ so that you are better equipped to build high-trust cultures as you move into more senior levels of executive responsibility.

In addition, whether your future is in higher management or not, you will discover great personal satisfaction in simply building a work unit around you where people find it a joy to work, which is exactly the case with Trust-Bonded Organizations™.

22

The HI-TRUST Formula: Humility

During the 1960s Mary Lawrence headed one of the most successful advertising firms in New York. Her company produced dozens of now-legendary commercials and taglines. Above the entrance to their headquarters, engraved in stone, were the words, "If we were humble, we would be perfect."

It was a modern twist on an old adage, usually traced to Benjamin Franklin, that humility is the one virtue which is impossible to attain. Once you achieve it, you celebrate by saying, "I've finally gained humility" – at which point you are no longer humble!

As these examples illustrate, humility is more likely to be a subject of jokes than a topic for serious consideration, especially in discussions of leadership. One notable exception is the attention Jim Collins calls to humility in his book *Good to Great*.

Examining the common denominators among CEOs who took companies from solid performers to enduring pace-setters, Collins cites the pivotal role of humility in their style of leadership. The widespread popularity of Collins' book has thus sparked countless follow-on discussions of humility in leadership.

Still, with all the interest that Collins has aroused, the topic of humility finds little place in management and leadership literature. To demonstrate this deficiency, simply perform a web search on a phrase like "leadership and humility."

The vast majority of the first 100 hits will come from one of two sources. They will either be reviews of Collins' work. Or they will be articles which apply what Jesus taught about humility to leadership. Moreover, most of the applications in this second category center on religious and spiritual leadership, not leadership roles in business or institutional life.

Why this neglect of humility in leadership literature? In part it's because our Western models of leadership have their roots in Greek and Roman culture, where humility was hardly a virtue. For the Greeks, being a "real man" (the Greeks and Romans never thought of leadership in terms of women) meant being so tough and strong that you always settled things on your own terms.

Thus, even though the Greeks wrote extensively on ethics, none of these works praised forgiveness as a manly quality. Forgiveness was viewed as weakness. Real men did not forgive. They exacted revenge.

To Greeks there was no finer exemplar of "being a man" than Ulysses. Returning from his decade-long odyssey, he mercilessly slaughtered the men who, presuming him dead, had pursued the hand of his wife. Ulysses was clearly not inclined to "turn the other cheek," to borrow from the language of Jesus.

Indeed, Christianity's emphasis on mercy, forgiveness, and humility added to the disdain with which Romans greeted this new-fangled religion. Not that the Greco-Roman world discounted humility altogether. After all, Greek theater supplied oft-told tales of overweening pride that led to tragic results. But these dramatic themes aimed more at warning against unchecked arrogance than at purposefully promoting humility.

In time, of course, the Christian ethic prevailed and continues to shape the modern world, as it did the medieval world. Business ethics, for example, are largely an extension of principles from Jesus, Moses, and the Hebrew prophets. It's therefore easy to presume that our models of leadership are drawn from Christian precedents.

But our concept of leadership per se owes much more to the Greeks and Romans than to Jesus. Leadership is typically described in terms of winning, not serving. In terms of "taking charge," not collaborating. In terms of glorious achievement, not humble appreciation for the opportunity to serve.

The absence of humility inevitably limits the potential for trust-building.

Little wonder, then, that humility finds only limited space in contemporary works on leadership. Yet, for Trust-Centered Leadership™ humility is vital. We rarely trust people who are arrogant, boastful, and self-centered. Nor do we trust people who refuse to acknowledge their mistakes or learn from their miscues. The absence of humility inevitably limits the potential for trust-building.

The word "humility" itself comes from the Latin word *humus*, which means "dirt" or "earth." Behind the concept of humility is the realization that life inevitably ends with a return to the earth – "from dust to dust," as the expression goes. Since this inglorious end awaits all of us, it hardly behooves us to be boastful or full of ourselves. Ultimately we all turn into dust.

True humility never lets us lose sight of our human mortality with all of its limitations. Humility keeps us attuned to our frailty, our inadequacy, and our vulnerability. It therefore keeps ego in balance. Humility is the "golden mean" (to borrow from Aristotle) between arrogance and conceit on one side and an anemic existence with no strength of ego on the other.

I find, however, that people commonly fail to recognize humility as this kind of middle ground. Because I speak so often about humility as vital to Trust-Centered Leadership™, I regularly ask my audience what it means, from their perspective, to say that a person is humble. As often as not they respond by picturing a personality that is docile, acquiescent, and reluctant to exert itself or take a stand.

None of these qualities, of course, are traits we seek in leaders. If this is the way we view humility, then it's little wonder that "being humble" is not an attribute we readily associate with strong leadership. Moreover, the frequency with which I receive this type of response convinces me that humility may be the most misunderstood virtue in our language.

Truth be told, genuine humility requires both a healthy ego and tremendous personal strength of character. Some of the world's most effective leaders, indeed, have been noted for their humility. In our own history men like George Washington and Abraham Lincoln come to mind. Once the Treaty of Paris was signed, ending the American War for Independence, King George III of England asked his ministers, "What will George Washington do now?" The king presumed that Washington would follow the pattern of historic revolutionaries and conquerors and would therefore make himself king.

Genuine humility requires both a healthy ego and tremendous personal strength of character.

To the monarch's surprise, his advisors answered, "Washington will go back to Virginia and become a farmer again."

"If that's true," the king replied, "he is the most humble man on earth." A few weeks later Washington was back at Mount Vernon, running his farm.

Despite the Greek and Roman low regard for humility, the ancient world, too, had exemplars of this virtue. Perhaps there is no more striking example than Moses, whose impact on history is rivaled by only a handful of others. Yet the Bible describes him as the most humble man of his era.

This is a telling statement, given the Bible's elevation of humility as a core value. If Moses, with his record of decisive achievement, exemplifies the Biblical concept of an humble leader, then humility is far-removed from a namby-pamby, weak-kneed approach to life.

The root meaning of humility makes its way into phrases such as "an humble village" or someone's "humble beginnings." Here the word "humble" clearly conveys the sense of being unpretentious. Humility is primarily an unpretentious attitude toward life and our relationships with others. We are not puffed up with our own self-importance. We don't act like the world revolves around us. We don't react defensively when caught in a miscue.

We hear a call for being unpretentious when people say that they want leaders who are "truly authentic." Stripped of all of its nuances, "being authentic" basically boils down to having no pretense. This very lack of pretense helps people feel more comfortable in being open, candid, and truthful with their leader. It also accelerates the pace at which they build trust in those who lead them.[47]

For the leader who wants to enjoy high trust, personal humility returns exceptional dividends:

- Humility lets us dismiss concerns about being the center of attention, so that we can step aside and let others shine. People don't tend to trust people who insist on taking all the credit or hogging the spotlight.

- Humility leaves us open to what others can teach us, no matter what their station in life. As a result we learn and develop wisdom more quickly, because we let everyone be our mentor.

---

[47] For a thorough treatment of authenticity in the person of the leader, see Rob Gofee and Gareth Jones, "Managing Authenticity: The Paradox of Great Leadership," *Harvard Business Review* (December 2005), pp. 86-94. Jack and Suzy Welch have described being "real" and "authentic" as a leader as "the most powerful thing you can do," adding that authenticity is "the foundation" of leadership effectiveness. "Get Real, Get Ahead," *Business Week* (May 14, 2007), p. 100.

- Humility lets us treat even difficult people with such respect that we help them feel worthwhile. Again, people do not typically invest their trust in someone who makes them feel invisible or insignificant.

- Humility preserves a spirit of gratitude. A spirit of gratitude does more than perhaps any other character trait to keep our outlook on life positive and healthy. Sensing this, people are unlikely to put great trust in a leader who is ungrateful, for (unconsciously, at least) they realize that ingratitude is a sign of other character flaws.

- Humility allows us to confront our own failings and take valuable lessons from them. Nothing is more harmful to trust than a leader who lives in denial or who never learns from things done poorly.

- Humility allows us to be more patient with those who are still learning and thus prone to mistakes. We see in them a reflection of our own need to learn and improve. Appropriate patience is critical in building trust, for impatience breeds anxiety and even fear among those we lead, the very antithesis of trust.

- Humility makes us approachable and receptive to being held accountable. Accountability is essential for any High-Trust, Peak-Performance Organization. But accountability must work both ways. Leaders who hold others accountable must be open and willing to be held accountable themselves. Otherwise, a double standard is at work that is inimical to trust.

- Humility keeps our curiosity alive. Aware of how much we don't know, recognizing that we have our own pattern of blind spots, we are eager to explore and learn. After all, people don't normally trust "know-it-alls."

As you review this list of ways in which humility contributes to trust-building, you will notice that many of them relate to learning.

Learning from others. Learning from mistakes. Learning from being held accountable. Learning by keeping curiosity high.

It's this distinct relationship between humility and learning that makes humility so critical for leaders who would propel an organization to sustained peak performance. In the opening pages of this book we noted the similarity between the qualities of a high-trust culture and the characteristics of what Peter Senge calls a "learning organization."

If, as Senge contends, the organization that learns most quickly is the one that makes itself most competitive, then leaders with genuine humility are essential to competitive advantage.

23

The HI-TRUST Formula: Integrity

I t's all but impossible to discuss the qualities of trusted leadership without talking about integrity from the outset. In the absence of integrity other elements of the HI-TRUST formula wither in their potential to be trust-builders.

Integrity is itself an intriguing word, given its numerous shades of meaning. Its root, of course, is the word "integer," which refers to a whole number. Anything with integrity is singular. It's not half this and half something else. Integrity implies consistency throughout.

But integrity also carries the meaning of being sound, dependable. When an engineer speaks of a bridge or building as having integrity, we can be assured that the structure is in no danger of collapse.

Less commonly integrity carries the sense of adhering to a set of conventions or standards. An art work has integrity if it is consistent with the norms for that particular genre of art. In science, findings that ignore the scientific method are considered lacking in integrity.

Then, of course, there is the lead definition of integrity in the Oxford English Dictionary, which describes it as "the quality of being honest and morally upright."

The common denominator in all of these concepts is a thoroughgoing consistency organized around some underlying standard. Integrity, in its most fundamental sense, connotes a consistent essence.

- The integrity of a bridge or building implies that the structure's support system is consistent with design specifications.

- Artistic and scientific integrity entails consistency with established protocols.

- Moral and ethical integrity is consistency with a code of values.

Consistency and standards. These two factors are the bookends that frame integrity. And here, in this combination of consistency and standards, is the link that makes trust and integrity inseparable. Trust, as we've defined it, is "complete confidence that a person or organization will consistently do what is right." And to "consistently do what is right" is to practice integrity.

Integrity is our primary measure for determining strength of character.

This linkage between integrity and trust is particularly important in the realm of character. Trust, we have seen, coalesces either around character, performance, or both. Trust in a person's character is no assurance that we also trust the person's ability to perform. The reverse is equally true. We may trust performance, but not character. Drawing on this distinction in chapter eleven, we identified character and performance as the two primary domains of trust.

Within these domains, integrity is our primary measure for determining strength of character. And this is what makes integrity non-negotiable for leadership. Warren Bennis, who studied more than 150 leaders over a decade and a half, determined that "character is the key to leadership." He backs up his conclusion with research from Harvard indicating that 85% of a leader's performance is a product of personal character."[48]

If this is true, then even performance (the second domain of trust) is largely dependent on character, the first domain of trust. Performance demands technical competence, interpersonal skills, and organizational savvy, to be sure. But the linchpin to performance is character.

Interestingly, "performance" has a verb behind it. (My "performance" is the result of how I "perform.") But there is no verb behind either integrity or character. We don't speak of "doing" integrity or "doing" character. We can only speak of them as something we possess. Something we have. What we do (performance) flows from what we are (character).

Moreover, character and integrity are so closely intertwined that when people lack integrity we say that they "don't have much character." Not having character suggests one of two possibilities. Either the person has improper standards. Or the person has appropriate standards, but fails to live up to them.

In either case there is an integrity issue. And in neither case are we likely to see this individual as trustworthy in the domain of character.

The beginning point for integrity, then, is to have appropriate standards. The standards behind integrity take a variety of forms.

- Some standards are values.

- Others are principles that guide us.

- Still others are beliefs that spell out our worldview.

These three – values, principles, and beliefs – form a hierarchy in which there is a logical progression from values to principles to

---

[48] Warren Bennis, "The Leadership Advantage," Leader to Leader Institute, Spring, 1999, 3.

beliefs. For purposes of shorthand, we will call this the VPB hierarchy.

- Values reside at the top of this hierarchy. They shape everything below them.

- Each value gives rise to one or more principles, whose purpose is to support the values they serve.

- Each principle, in turn, gives rise to one or more beliefs that explain why we hold the principle to be vital.

It's not uncommon to hear the words "values," "principles," and "beliefs" used rather interchangeably. Some people call honesty a value, others call it a principle. Another person might cast it in the form a belief by saying, "I believe in honesty."

So what is honesty? A value? A principle? Or is it an object of belief?

As we use the terms in the VPB hierarchy, honesty is a value. Then certain principles (such as "telling the truth") are logical extensions of the value "honesty." And the principle of telling the truth telling is supported by certain beliefs, one of which might be, "Honesty is the best policy."

Let's delve deeper into these distinctions by examining the meaning of values, principles, and beliefs in the VPB hierarchy. In my judgment the most helpful way to think of values is to borrow from the field of neuro-linguistic programming (NLP), which describes values as "things we move toward or away from."

Values, in other words, are the basis of our entire motivational system, since what ultimately motivates our actions (apart from reflex reactions) are things we want to acquire or attain (move toward) or things we want to avoid (move away from).

Now, looking at values this way is something of a departure from day-to-day conversations about values. If someone asks us to identify our values, we are likely to include only things that we strive for, e.g., justice, harmony, peace. These are all things we move toward.

But when we expand our definition of values to include things we move away from, our list of values might now include such things as failure, poverty, or guilt.

The reason I prefer this broader view of values is that it brings greater precision to discussions of motivation. As leaders, we quickly learn that people are motivated both by what they want (such as "recognition") and what they don't want ("blame," for example).

By defining values as what people move away from as well as what they move toward, we have a simple framework in which to analyze motivational patterns.

Values are such powerful motivators, indeed, that they can override reflex responses and impulses. The strongest impulse in our make-up, originating in the deepest structures of the brain, is the instinct to survive.

Yet people routinely set this instinct aside by risking life itself to rescue someone in danger. If asked what motivated them to hazard such risk, they will answer either in terms of a value or in terms of a principle that points to a value.

So our first distinction is that values are the ultimate source of our motivation. Second, values can always be stated as a single word ("love," "achievement," "unpleasantness") or a short phrase ("customer service," "financial security"). Notice that these are noun constructions exclusively. They have no verbal components. No qualifying adverbs. No quantifying adjectives. Values are static. And they are stated as abstract nouns in terms like achievement, service, or security.

Occasionally we join a brief descriptor to this abstract noun to narrow the scope of abstraction. Love of country. Pride of ownership. Customer service. Financial security. These "scope-limiters" answer the question, "Within what realm?"

Thus, when we list customer service among our values, "customer" answers the question, "Service in what realm?" Similarly, if we name financial security as a value, "financial" answers the question, "Security in what realm?"

Apart from these scope-limiters, values stand unadorned as pure abstract nouns, connoting things we move toward or away from. Once we begin quantifying or qualifying a value further, we move from values to principles.

The purpose of principles is to give us guidelines for implementing our values. We feel answerable to principles, because they describe what we see as appropriate and inappropriate ways to put our values into practice.

For instance, one supporting principle might be "timely response to customer complaints." Another principle could be "minimizing the time in line at checkout stations" or "maintaining industry-leading customer service."

As these examples illustrate, we can express principles in brief phrases, just as we do with values, but the phrase is slightly longer. This is because principles, by providing guidelines, require more specific and quantifiable language. Whereas values are stated as abstract nouns, the wording of principles may include verbal elements (*minimizing* the time in line at checkout stations") or adverbs and adjectives (*timely* response to customer complaints").

The role of beliefs is to state the specific rationale behind our principles. Beliefs explain why we have chosen particular principles and why we prioritize them as we do. One team of authors calls beliefs "the 'executive summary' of our world view."[49] While we can

---

[49] Doug Lennick and Fred Kiel, *Moral Intelligence: Enhancing Business Performance and Leadership Success* (Philadelphia: Wharton School of Publishing, 2005), p. 49.

express values and principles in only a phrase or two, it takes a complete sentence to state a belief.

To illustrate, one of your corporate values might be employee retention. Next, certain principles would support this value. These principles might include treating employees respectfully, offering employees exceptional personal development opportunities, or providing on-site childcare for employees with small children.

Each principle is then expressed through a series of beliefs. One such belief might be, "Employees are more loyal when they know we will help them develop personal skills and abilities."

Because they lay out the rationale for our principles, beliefs are cognitive in nature. They build on logic, data, information, and reflection on experience.

Values, by contrast, are affective in nature. They reside in that part of our being where we form our likes and our dislikes. The VPB hierarchy therefore encompasses both the affective and cognitive portions of our inner being. In addition, the VPB hierarchy, properly developed, aligns our affective and cognitive outlooks to provide a roadmap for living life.

Integrity thus begins with a set of standards that include an integrated set of values, principles and beliefs. Appropriate standards, whether personal or corporate, meet the following litmus tests:

- **They are coherent.** Collectively our standards fit together as a natural and cogent unit, properly prioritized, with no contradictions among them.

  - First, there is no contradiction within each level of the VPB hierarchy. That is, beliefs do not contradict beliefs. Principles do not contradict principles. Values do not contradict values.

  - Second, the levels themselves are non-contradictory. Beliefs do not contradict principles, nor do principles contradict values.

- **They are applicable across all contexts.** That is, our standards are universal enough that there is no need to modify them from setting to setting. They are reliable guides, whatever the circumstance. This does not mean that we prioritize our values exactly the same in every context. After all, none of us is likely to prioritize values the same way in our family life that we do in our business life. But these shifts represent only a realignment of priorities, not the abandonment of one set of values, principles, and beliefs for another.

- **They globalize to the betterment of all.** In other words, overall human well-being would be well served if every person in the world chose to live by these standards. Some call this the "ecology test." Appropriate standards, whether they are values, principles, or beliefs, should always lead to a triple win – a win for the person who holds the standards, a win for others with whom this person interacts, and a win for the overall well-being of our planet and the human race.

When asked for an example of integrity in practice, I often cite what happened with one of my clients on a cross-country flight. At the time he was part of a team developing a project potentially worth billions of dollars.

The Federal government would be the initial buyer. But the product had even broader application in the commercial world. His company was one of three corporations designing prototypes to secure the government contract.

On this particular day he cashed in some frequent flyer miles and upgraded to first class. Boarding the plane, he took his seat on the second row behind two businessmen traveling together in row ahead of him.

He had never met either of these men and did not recognize their faces. But shortly after takeoff, their conversation led him to a surprising discovery.

These men, it turned out, worked for one of the other companies in the competition. Not only that, they were in charge of the prototype that their firm was building. One man headed the project. The other was his recently-named successor, slated to take over the project in just a matter of weeks.

Fifteen minutes into the flight the first man reclined his seat, broke out a laptop computer, and said, "This would be a great opportunity for me to take you through the nuts and bolts of the project."

He then brought up an opening screen, a full-color drawing of his company's proposed design. The reclined seat gave my client an unobstructed view of the computer, and he could hear the man's commentary without missing a word.

If you were my client, how would you react to this set of circumstances. One viewpoint would argue, "What great luck!! Here's an opportunity to get all the details on our competition's game plan." Imagine how valuable this piece of intelligence could be to everyone from designers to marketing specialists to contract negotiators! What's more, bringing home this treasure trove of information could mean a healthy bonus or even a promotion.

But my client worked for a company that elevates the importance of integrity – not merely internal integrity or integrity with customers, but integrity across the board. It was one of the primary reasons he had chosen to work for this particular company. What, then, did the standard of absolute integrity require?

To him the answer became clear when he asked himself, "What if the roles were reversed? What if one of these men were seated behind me and I was the one having this conversation with a co-worker? What would I want him to do?"

Posing these questions to himself, it took only a moment of reflection before he settled on a straightforward course of action. He pulled out one of his business cards, reached between the seats, offered it to the man with the computer, and said, "Before you continue, you might want to know who is sitting behind you."

The man looked at the card, turned to my client with a startled glance, thanked him profusely, then put the computer away.

Integrity means always doing right by people. Even at the cost of sacrificing personal self-interest or financial advantage. "Doing right by people" is how our personal VPB hierarchy meets the test of "globalizing to the betterment of all." It's how we create a win-win-win.

Integrity means always doing right by people.

But when the stakes are high, as they were that day on the airplane, integrity is put to its greatest test. In high-stake circumstances it's always tempting to rationalize a compromise on our standards.

For my client, however, compromise simply meant that there was a price on his integrity. Once we put a price tag on our integrity, we simultaneously cap our potential for building High-Trust, Peak-Performance Organizations.

Still, the temptation to cut corners on integrity is forever present, especially when significant financial advantage is in the equation. I faced this temptation recently myself when I began hiring employees in Ukraine.

Under Ukrainian law, employers are levied a hefty annual tax on salary payments. To get around this onerous tax burden, companies in Ukraine routinely declare an employee's salary at the mandated minimum wage, pay taxes on that amount, then slip additional cash payments to the employee off the books.

As we enlarge our staff in Ukraine, we would put ourselves in a far more advantageous position financially to conform to this prevailing practice. On the other hand, we want our employees to act ethically and watch out for our interests on every turn. How can we expect them to act with integrity if we are compromising on our own integrity in the way we pay them?

I also faced the temptation to compromise on integrity as I worked to rescue the college. As I mentioned in chapter one, we had lost a third of our enrollment in the two years before I became president. We needed students desperately.

Yet, on more than one occasion I urged parents who were ready to send a child to our campus to consider another alternative. I pointed them to other schools whose climate and academic offerings were far more conducive to their child's needs and aspirations. To "do right" by their son or daughter, this was the only proper course of action open to me.

Was this recommendation easy to make? Not always. I knew how much we could use the revenue from the student's tuition, room, and board. I also knew people on campus who would question my sanity for turning away a prospective enrollee. Even the families themselves were usually a bit surprised that I would recommend a different college for their child.

But because of the integrity behind my actions, these same families endorsed the school enthusiastically to other people, who in turn became financial supporters and who sent their own children to our campus.

On a larger scale a man with whom I would later work as a consultant did something similar as a regional marketing executive for one of America's most recognized firms. Their equipment was commonplace in corporations big and small, and the equipment was serviced on site.

He trained service technicians to do more than simply repair equipment. He taught them to interact with customers in ways that would identify other needs which his company's product lines might meet. At the time this was a rather new approach to marketing, although others were also pioneering it.

But he added a unique twist. He told his representatives, "If you see that some other company's product is a notably better match for the customer's needs than ours, point the customer to that product."

As you might imagine, management above him was hardly enamored with this approach. But it proved its wisdom in only a few short months. Companies soon learned that his representatives would recommend what was best for the customer, not what was best for meeting sales quotas.

Not surprisingly, customers developed a special bond of trust with his field representatives. These companies then made it a practice to call his people first when considering the purchase of new equipment. As a result, having positioned himself to get the first shot at a customer's business, he moved sales to notably higher levels.

When I tell this story, people immediately see my friend's wisdom. After all, his integrity made money both for him and his company.

But when I tell the story about my client on the airplane, I sometimes get a different response. My audience commonly questions his judgment. They reason along these lines: "He should have taken advantage of the situation. He had a bird's nest on the ground. I dare say that neither of those other men would have spoken up if they had been in his position. No, they would have stayed quiet and made lots of notes."

Integrity, however, is not a measure of what other people would do if they were in our shoes. They are not in our shoes. We are. If we only feel obligated to practice integrity with those who reciprocate in kind, then we are acting as though integrity is conditional.

But "conditional integrity" is a contradiction in terms. By its very nature integrity is always non-conditional.

And being non-conditional, integrity holds its own course, even when others take advantage of it. Even when treated unfairly. Even in the face of an inner urge to exact revenge or retribution.

Integrity is never for sale. If we treat people with integrity only if they are people of integrity themselves, our own integrity is no longer unconditional. Instead, our integrity wears a price tag. The price tag is not financial. But it's a price tag, nonetheless. It reads, "If you are willing to barter, just treat me with integrity, and I will do the same for you. Otherwise, all bets are off."

In the early 1980s I established a friendship with a brilliant artist who ran one of the nation's most successful graphics arts studios. I'll call him Eric. His shop produced album covers and movie posters for the most respected names in the entertainment world. In addition, he had once been a "go to" guy for sexually oriented magazines that wanted quality touch-ups done on photo layouts.

Integrity is never for sale. Not at any price.

As success built, Eric's life and values changed. He became a family man, a loving father, and a devout Christian. With his new VPB hierarchy, he decided to move out of the pornography trade. It did not align with his new values. Once he made his decision, he acted immediately, even though he was giving up a major piece of revenue.

Then, a couple of years later, one of his former customers called in a panic. "We are in a huge bind," the man said. "The press is ready to roll on our new issue, and we've just discovered we don't have the legal rights to some of the pictures we were going to use. We've got to substitute several new photos that have not been touched up. I know you're not doing this kind of work anymore, but could you make an exception and do just one rush job for us?"

"No," Eric replied. "I'm not available."

The man shot back, "But we'll pay you $75,000 just to do this one job for us."

Eric again declined. The man went to $125,000. The answer was still "no."

Finally the man said, "Okay, Eric, I'll just cut to the chase. I've been authorized to go as high as $200,000 if you will do this."

Growing tired of the pointless conversation, Eric snapped, "I won't do it for two hundred thousand dollars. And I won't do it for two million dollars." The other man, clearly stunned, came back with an incredulous, "Why not?"

Eric answered in a simple and matter of fact tone, "Let's just say that I don't like the demeaning way in which your magazine exploits women as disposable sex objects."

There was a long silence on the other end of the phone. Finally the man said, "You know, Eric, there are days when I'm not too crazy about it myself," then added a quick goodbye. His magazine never called again.

Integrity is never for sale. Not at any price.

24

The HI-TRUST Formula:
Truth

A s an essential for building trust, truth ranks second only to integrity. Integrity, of course, implies telling the truth. But truth, as a builder of trust, goes beyond the simple but sometimes difficult task of being honest in what we say.

To build genuine, effective trust we must be equally willing to hear the truth. To confront the truth. To keep the organization and its culture grounded in truth and reality.

My friend Juanell Teague has a personal motto she tags to the signature line of her emails. It says simply, "Tell the truth quicker, faster." As one of the nation's foremost consultants for professional speakers, she has learned that truth postponed is improvement delayed. So long as we skirt the truth or avoid its unpleasant implications, we are reduced to a game of pretense and half-truths that dilute or even destroy effectiveness.

High-performance cultures can afford nothing less than a culture of truth. Peak performance in any organization demands free-flowing feedback loops. To stay ahead of the pack, we must tell the truth quicker, faster.

When I became a college president, I made this very point in my first meeting with the executive committee. "You will never endanger your job or your working relationship with me by bringing me bad news," I said. "You *will* risk your job, however, by blowing smoke at me or keeping me in the dark about something I need to know. Until I know the truth, I can't make an appropriate response. Our finances right now are so precarious that I can't afford to waste a penny. So I always need to know the truth, I need to know it fully, and I need to know it quickly."

The ancient Persians had a custom that no one was to appear before the emperor wearing a sad face. The penalty could sometimes be death. In the emperor's presence you were to act as though everything were pleasant, even when it was not.

This old Persian custom still prevails in many organizations, where no one dares state bad news openly, especially to "the head honcho." In these types of organizations fear is the most frequent deterrent to truth-telling. Apparently many top executives have never learned that a climate of fear, far from making them stronger, actually leaves them more vulnerable. It hides truth from them.

History itself warns of this vulnerability. Dictators who rule through fear are often purposefully misled about pivotal developments, because people are too frightened to tell them the truth. Two noted examples are Adolf Hitler and Saddam Hussein, who created such pervasive fear that even their closest advisors were not honest with them about the collapsing fortunes of their armies.

Unfortunately, fear of being truthful with "the head honcho" generalizes in such a way that people are hesitant to be truthful to anyone in upper management. If you find yourself in a leadership post in an organization where management above you evokes fear and trembling, you probably are not being told the truth yourself, no matter how much people like you personally. You must counter self-protecting communication by going the extra mile to ferret out truth.

During my Navy enlisted years, our base was assigned a new commanding officer who took pride in managing by means of fear.

He bellowed. He ranted. He cursed out senior officers in front of their staffs. In essence he had perfected the art of being a bully and a boor. Within a month of his arrival, morale on the base plummeted and never recovered until long after he retired.

His executive officer, a very decent and caring man, knew that in this climate of fear, people were afraid to tell him things that he needed to know. He was also aware that my duties put me in a unique position to interact with almost every department on base.

So once or twice a month, when he and I were both working late, he would come around to my office, coffee cup in hand, sit down across the desk from me, prop his feet on the front of my desk, lean back in his chair, and say, "What's going on around here that people are afraid to tell me about?"

In the absence of a culture of truth, a culture of trust is impossible.

Because I worked only thirty paces from his office, I knew him well and trusted his genuine concern for the command and for its enlisted personnel. But I was virtually alone in my conviction. Elsewhere in the organization people projected the same negative feelings on him that they had for the commanding officer. They were afraid to be candid with him. Had he not gone out of his way to uncover the truth, he would have been left without knowledge and insight he sorely needed.

The commanding officer's overbearing, brutish style undercut trust in two telling dimensions. First, as is always the case with fear-based management styles, he launched a frontal attack on trust. In terms of character and interpersonal relationships, we don't trust people whom we fear. Second, it was general knowledge on base that no one was telling him the full truth. And it's genuinely difficult to trust a leader whom you know to be misinformed.

In the absence of a culture of truth, a culture of trust is impossible. Trust-Centered Leadership™ has no greater priority than creating an environment in which truth flows openly and freely. This begins with leaders like you who model truth-telling and have the integrity to stick with it.

People come to trust you by watching you in action. They especially watch to see if you tell the truth. Consistently. Openly. Even when the truth is unpleasant. Even when truth puts you in a bad light.

There are dozens of ways to be untruthful. The most obvious one is lying. Others are more subtle and don't tend to be classified in the same category as overt dishonesty or deception. But they are equally damaging to a culture of truth. Some of the more common culprits are:

- telling a half-truth

- exaggerating personal accomplishments

- taking undue credit

- projecting a false image of being "in the know" or being well-connected in prestigious circles

- letting misrepresentations go unchallenged

- using spin to distort the facts

- word-smithing to hide details that are unflattering, unpleasant, or potentially discrediting

- purposefully leaving false impressions

- making promises without a genuine commitment to fulfill them

- blaming others to avoid personal scrutiny

- using vague language to invite wrong conclusions

You can doubtlessly add other items to this list. The common denominator in all of them is knowingly separating what we communicate from an accurate portrayal of reality.

This does not mean that leaders must divulge every detail in order to be truthful. But it does mean that Trust-Centered Leadership™ never intentionally uses communication to mislead.

Interestingly, when I present this list of culprits as trust-busting behavior, I'm no longer surprised to spark a disagreement. Some people will insist that "spin" and words carefully chosen to blur or mask the truth are simply shrewd and savvy techniques for achieving your objective. In other words, unless a statement is blatantly deceptive, it's not a violation of truth.

This narrow definition of truth-telling is a natural outgrowth of trends in popular culture over the past fifty years. These decades have assaulted the very concept of truth itself, particularly the idea of universal truth.

It has been replaced with a definition of truth that is totally subjective in nature. By this new standard of truth "what is true for you is not necessarily true for me."

In the 1970s I heard Francis Schaeffer, the noted philosopher and theologian, use the term "true truth." When asked about this awkward phrase, he said that lectures to university students had reduced him to speaking in this manner.

Many students, he explained, treated all truth as subjective. So he had resorted to "true truth" as a way of describing truth that is something more than mere personal perspective.

In the years since his comment the meaning of truth has continued to erode. Along with it, moral and ethical codes have become increasingly relativistic. After all, if there is no truth that is certain, there are no rights and wrongs that are certain.

Interestingly, however, even among the most relativistic thinkers, only a pure Machiavellian defends hypocrisy. Today few indictments are more stinging than to be called "a hypocrite."

This attests to the fact that, despite all the word games with 'truth," we have a universal consensus that statements should align closely with reality. And this is also why leaders who shave the truth lose respect and trust, even in an age of relativistic morality,

---

A solid reputation for truth-telling serves us especially well in those moments which all leaders face when we must purposefully withhold information from our people. Or when we must defend unpopular decisions by saying, "I'm not free to go into the details."

When someone is particularly distraught with a decision, they may interpret "I'm not free to go into the details" as stonewalling, ducking the truth, or a cover-up. And as leaders we have little power to disarm this conviction once it takes shape in the minds of observers. But if leaders have established a stalwart record for telling the truth, people are more likely to give them the benefit of the doubt when details must be closely held.

We have all heard leaders say, "Trust me on this." And we have probably uttered the words ourselves. Yet, no matter how respectfully we make the request, people may refuse to comply.

Moreover, when they do in fact choose to trust us and give us the benefit of the doubt, their choice has little to do with our request. Instead, they grant us the benefit of the doubt because they have watched us in action and know that we have an absolutely consistent record for integrity and truth-telling.

Truthful, straightforward communication is essential if an organization is to stay grounded in reality. Without straightforward communication, trust in leadership will remain limited. People don't trust fully when they suspect that they are being doled out a dish of selective truth.

Newly elected politicians in both major parties usually attend a "charm school" that teaches them, among other things, how to bob and weave artfully when answering a question. In confidential, "off-the-record" conversations I've even had national political figures spell out their specific techniques for seeming to answer a question without really answering it. Then they wonder why public trust in politicians is so low!!

It's no accident that the word "spin" first became popularly associated with political speech. Political figures are so frequently blatant in their use of spin that ordinary citizens are becoming astute at recognizing it when it happens. And people are now just as quick to suspect spin in corporate life as they are in political life.

People don't trust fully when they suspect that they are being doled out a dish of selective truth.

Few things are more disarming, therefore, or a greater contributor to trust, than a leader who speaks straightforwardly. A leader who is upfront with people. Who avoids spin and slanted reporting. Who never sugar-coats things to make himself or herself look good. Who lays things out as they really are and deals with them realistically.

But be forewarned, depending on the history you inherit, straightforward communication may initially impair trust, not improve it. If people are not used to experiencing this kind of openness, they may not know what to make of it.

When I took over the helm of the college, I recognized an urgent need for straightforward communication, particularly about our finances, which were worsening by the month. People knew things were bad financially. After all, payrolls had been missed routinely of late.

But no one outside of the business office knew any details about our true financial condition. Consequently, the campus was rife with speculation, anxiety, and suspicion.

Compounding the problem was the leadership style of the president who preceded me. A legendary educator, he was the only person in the history of American education to lead three different colleges from non-accredited to fully accredited status. And his integrity was unexcelled and unquestioned.

But as a CEO he had one serious short-coming. He simply had no head for money. The school's accounting systems were a mystery to him. So when he spoke to the campus community about finances, he never went beyond broad generalities.

I felt compelled to break that pattern of communication. "If I'm going to ask these people to stick with me," I decided, "they deserve to know what the real score is."

So for the first month on campus I spent my evenings with records from the finance office, poring over the books. When I finally had a handle on things, I announced that I was planning a series of monthly meetings, open to all employees and their spouses. I also explained that I would use these meetings to lay out our finances in detail and offer my best cash flow estimates for the next 60 days.

When I announced this plan, some on my executive team objected vehemently. "You'll only destroy morale," they insisted (as though there was much morale left to destroy). "No," I answered, "the truth may be unpleasant. But whatever damage it does will be far less harmful than keeping people in the dark."

The first meeting was well-attended, with almost 100% participation. I did my utmost to answer every question candidly. And what happened to morale? In several cases it dropped like a rock, just as my objectors had warned. But it dropped for reasons you might not anticipate.

It turned out that people were not sure how to handle this new openness. They found it hard to believe that they were being told the entire truth. Conversations among faculty and staff went something like this: "The administration never told us anything before, and things were bad. So, if they are now telling us how bad things are, what they are *not* telling us must REALLY be bad."

Gradually, however, as I held course with my meetings, the doubters became convinced that nothing was being hidden. They were being told the truth fully and straightforwardly. And with that recognition their morale turned and actually surged upward.

Straightforward communication must also extend to account-ability and evaluations of performance. Recently the board of a non-profit organization asked me to meet with them to discuss a key player in their organization whose performance was substandard. Some had already made up their minds to dismiss him. Others felt that with coaching he could be rescued. They wanted to know my opinion.

"How long have you had misgivings about his performance?" I opened.

"Well, we actually had a vote of no-confidence in him three years ago," came the reply. (Unfortunately, the non-profit world is notorious for leaving underperformers in place long after the for-profit world would have let them go.)

I then asked, "How many job reviews has he had since then?"

"We've reviewed him every year."

"And does he know about the vote of no-confidence?" I contin-ued.

"No," they acknowledged.

"Even though you never told him about the no-confidence vote, did you address with him candidly the factors that led to your vote?" This time the answer was a "yes," followed immediately by a long, reflective pause. Finally one board member looked around the room and said, "Let's be honest. We didn't really level with him. We sugar-coated the message so much that I'm not sure he ever heard it."

Now, three years later, they were dealing with considerable dis-content within their staff and among themselves, primarily because they had chosen to be less than straightforward in reviewing his performance. Failure to maintain straightforward communication almost always comes back to haunt us.

Lest I seem to be picking on non-profits, let me hasten to add that I've seen this same type of failure in business. I think of two partners who started a business in a garage along with a woman who kept their records and handled administrative matters.

Five years later, the company had grown to 200 employees with a heavy manufacturing schedule. The woman was also still with them, still serving as their executive assistant. But her attitude and communication style were running off workers right and left. Turnover was driving recruiting and training costs through the roof.

The partners would not be straightforward with her about her conduct, however, for fear that she would walk out the door. Having been with the company from the beginning, she was the sole repository for critical corporate knowledge.

The partners were afraid that they could not get by without her expertise. The price they were paying, however, was a climate of distrust that was probably impacting their bottom line far more adversely than the cost of training someone to fill her role.

I consulted with another company that expended constant organizational energy "wiring around" a fairly senior member of the management team, whose people skills left much to be desired. Yet no one had ever leveled with him about his poor people skills. He had received fairly stellar performance reviews for years.

When I asked why, I was told that he was by far the company's most ingenious thinker in terms of new products. No one wanted to risk losing him to a competitor by being dealing with his management deficiencies straightforwardly.

When these kinds of situations go unchecked through repeated review cycles, they become especially difficult to deal with later. In each of the cases cited above, so much dissension had arisen around the problem employee that corrective action was no longer an option. Something had to be done, and soon.

But management found itself in a bind, for to tell the employee that past performance reviews had been less than straightforward was to acknowledge that management had also been less than truthful. And that's a difficult admission to make.

Moreover, even when management musters the courage to make this admission, there's no assurance that the employee will receive it well. Instead, the employee may shout from the rooftops about management "hypocrisy" in failing to be straightforward for months or even years.

We do more damage to trust by postponing the moment of truth than by putting truth respectfully on the table.

Other workers, who hear the disgruntled employee's tale, then start to wonder, "What about me? Are they doing the same thing to me? Are they giving me an honest appraisal of my performance?" These questions, in turn, undercut trust in the organization's basic integrity.

In the long-run we do more damage to trust by postponing the moment of truth than by putting truth respectfully on the table. Most people respect straightforwardness. No one respects what they see as deception or hypocrisy. For this reason, Juanell's adage serves us well. Tell the truth quicker, faster.

25

The HI-TRUST Formula: Responsiveness

The fourth element of the HI-TRUST formula is responsiveness. In Trust-Centered Leadership™ responsiveness is no less vital than telling the truth. To understand why, we need to return again to the SIRVU formula and the two principles of feeling respected and valued.

To feel respected and valued by their leaders, people must perceive the leader as genuinely concerned for them personally, for others whom they hold dear, and for things they treasure. In addition, people determine the depth of a leader's concern (and its genuineness) largely by monitoring his or her responsiveness.

The monitoring begins with the leader's responsiveness to them individually. Does the leader return their greetings warmly? Does their leader listen attentively when they speak? Does their leader seem eager to provide answers to their questions?

They next measure responsiveness in terms of how quickly the leader responds to needs and requests, as well as to troublesome circumstances that impact the organization. Is the leader assertive in the face of problems? Or passive? When a problem becomes known, how long does the leader wait before taking concrete action to address it? Can they count on the leader to make timely decisions? To take timely action? To raise timely questions?

Non-responsiveness on the part of a leader is always destructive of trust. When we are non-responsive as leaders, we leave the distinct impression that we are not truly concerned, either about our people personally or about the environment in which we ask them to work. In either case, our evident lack of concern raises questions about our good will, and hence our trustworthiness.

Responsiveness and responsibility are closely connected. Both connote a "response-ability." Responsiveness is a measure of how attuned we are to carrying out our responsibilities in a way that is timely, properly prioritized, respectful of others, and sensitive to common courtesies. In this regard I like the wording of the Oxford English Dictionary, which defines the term "responsive" as "responding readily and positively."

Non-responsiveness on the part of a leader is always destructive of trust.

When I think of responsiveness, I go back to my youth growing up in a rural community which had a volunteer fire department. Open pastures frequently caught fire during the hot, dry summer, and swept by high winds, fires could quickly threaten homes, not to mention livestock trapped behind barbed-wire fences. The key to preventing disaster was response time.

When the fire alarm went off (a wailing siren that could be heard from one end of town to the other), volunteer firemen everywhere dropped whatever they were doing, jumped in the nearest vehicle, and headed for the fire station. The first person there cranked up the engine of the pumper truck. As soon as two or three more joined him, they roared off toward the blaze.

Others, arriving minutes later, barreled out of the station in the remaining trucks, while still another group, unable to reach the station quickly, called the police dispatcher, got the location of the fire, and dashed there in personal vehicles. It was responsive improvisation at its best.

I can remember standing in my backyard as a teenager, battling flames away from the house with a water hose or pounding at them with wet burlap sacks and feeling the comforting assurance of fire truck sirens approaching quickly. Help was on the way.

Today, in my roles of leadership, I use those fire crews as a point of reference for what it means for me to be responsive myself. I have a certain bent toward perfectionism, which tempts me to delay action until I have a response that is as well-thought out, as well-informed, and as carefully articulated as possible.

All the while my people are wondering if help is on the way. As they wait for my response, trust is in the balance and my procrastination is not helping tilt the scale toward confidence.

Instead, my delay is opening the door for frustration with my inaction, speculation about my intention, or anxiety that perhaps nothing at all will be done. And none of these scenarios – frustration, speculation, and anxiety – is friendly toward trust.

By contrast, those firemen were more concerned with timely effectiveness than with perfection. They didn't wait for the best driver to be on scene before the fire engine roared out of the station. They didn't wait until every team was in place before they engaged the blaze. They simply went to work with the equipment and people at hand.

In my late twenties I did my first work as a consultant. I was hired by a chain of restaurants in the San Francisco Bay Area, owned by a close friend. Periodically managers would come by the owner's office to discuss particular problems in their stores.

He would listen to their description of the problem, then ask, "What action are you taking?" Commonly the reply was, "Well, I'm still thinking about the best way to handle the situation."

At this point the owner would gesture toward a sign on the wall behind his desk. The sign read, "It's very difficult to make mid-course corrections with a stationery object." This was his way of reminding himself, and his managers, to be responsive.

His leadership philosophy was that any action, so long as it is prefaced with a bit of reflection and wisdom, is better than no action at all. If nothing else, taking action serves to clarify solutions that don't work. That in itself is more information than was known before. Taking action can also surface options that were previously unnoticed.

On balance, however, he had found that timely responses, even when imperfect, are reasonably effective in most instances. When he implemented a solution, he never expected it to be unflawed.

To him taking action was simply the first step in a learning process in which feedback would lead to essential fine-tuning, to mid-course corrections, or to altogether new approaches. All the while, his managers and employees knew they could count on him to be responsive.

The owner himself was an ex-Marine. His "take action" manner had doubtlessly been shaped or reinforced by his service in the Corps. He would feel right at home with today's Marine doctrine for making decisions in the midst of battle. Its purpose is to maintain what the Marines describe as "decision momentum." The key to victory, they have concluded, is making timely decisions that keep pressing the action forward.

They therefore train battlefield decision-makers in what we might call the "70% solution." The principle is worded like this: if you have 70% of the information and you have done 70% of the analysis and you are 70% confident that the solution will work, go for it. More often than not, the Marines have found, battlefield actions that conform to this formula prove successful.

With the "70% solution" the Marines are acknowledging that critical decisions are often fraught with uncertainty and ambiguity. The goal of the "70% solution" is not to remove the ambiguity, but to reduce it to a level that the law of averages plays to the advantage of the decision-maker.

Being decisive and responsive in the face of ambiguity becomes more important the higher we go in management. One of the first lessons I learned as a new college president is that none of the easy decisions ever reached my desk. Other managers and executives were more than happy to resolve problems that offered straightforward solutions. The problems that came to me for resolution were those which involved pronounced risks, whatever my decision.

The same is true in any complex organization. As we climb the ladder of leadership, three realities become more pronounced at each rung of the ladder.

- First, the time horizons with which we work become longer.

- Second, our decisions have a greater and greater ripple effect on elements of the organization beyond our own.

- And third, the ambiguity in the options before us expands exponentially.

The CEO of one of America's largest companies once told me, "My greatest surprise in this role has been how little I can predict whether the choices I make will have any impact on the price of our stock, and if so, what the impact will be."

Another key by-product of our personal responsiveness as leaders is that it helps calm anxiety. When crisis looms or pivotal consequences are at stake, anxiety naturally rises within an organization. In times like these it is equally natural for people to look to their leader for cues as to how they should react themselves.

This almost instinctive "look-to-the-leader" response is programmed into us from childhood. Have you ever seen a toddler take a hard, but not particularly painful tumble, then look to a parent to see if the proper response is to cry or not?

We never quite outgrow this tendency. When we are in an uneasy situation, we tend to look around at the "veterans" and see how they are reacting. If they are showing concern, our own anxiety is likely to increase.

As leaders we cannot avoid being one of the "veterans" people look to for signals. I learned this firsthand as our financial crisis at the college grew larger. On a weekly, sometimes daily basis I met with the vice-president for finance to discuss cash flow.

The meeting was usually in his office, where we had more ready access to documents or reports we might need. Because all of the school's administrative offices fronted on a common hallway, and because my office and his were at opposite ends of the building, I had to walk by most of my management team en route to a powwow with the VP for finance.

One day, as I returned from his office and sat down at my desk, my secretary stepped in and quietly closed the door. "Everybody knows where you have just been," she said, "and they have a pretty good idea of what you were discussing. I just want you to know what a boost it is to morale when people see you coming back from one of those meetings walking with confidence and whistling a tune."

I was unprepared for her comment, because to that point I had never noticed that I whistled as I made my way down the hall. But I learned from her remark how important my personal resilience was in setting the tone of resilience for the entire organization.

Trust is about confidence. And people have little confidence in leaders who do not project confidence themselves. A leader's non-responsiveness to pressing difficulty leaves people to conclude one of three things.

- Either the leader is unconcerned about their well-being.
- Or the leader sees no solution to the predicament.
- Or the leader is merely overwhelmed and paralyzed.

Any of these perspectives erodes trust.

To this point we have focused on responsiveness as it relates to major challenges or problems before the organization. From the standpoint of leadership and trust-building, equally important is responsiveness in the form of what we might call common courtesies.

Trust is about confidence. And people have little confidence in leaders who do not project confidence themselves.

I've worked with some brilliant thinkers who excelled at wise, timely solutions, whatever the challenge, but who were not "people people" at all. Highly introverted leaders – especially the ones who love analysis and problem-solving – are particularly prone to showing a lack of people skills. Their introverted, problem-solving mindset leaves them unattuned to people around them, not to mention the emotional energy field running within the organization.

I realized this in myself because of helpful feedback from friends who said, "Do you know that you sometimes walk right past people in the hallway and don't even speak to them?" I couldn't believe them at first. But after hearing this from several sources, I not only had to accept it as true, I began monitoring myself more closely.

What I discovered is that I manifested this non-responsive behavior when I was minutes away from a speech or major presentation. To "psych myself up" I was going deep inside and starting to rehearse my opening remarks. In effect, I zoned out.

I became so inwardly focused that I could walk past my own children and not notice them. I quickly had to learn new ways of "psyching up" which did not convey a sense that I was disinterested in people or oblivious to their presence.

I had another telling experience about the same time that illustrated how important common courtesies are. The experience stemmed from a habit I had picked up years before as an enlisted man in the Navy.

One of my buddies was quite a prankster who loved to convince people that he was in fact British, even though he was serving in the U.S. Navy. His British accent was flawless. And as part of his act he would regularly address women as "my lady," although he pronounced it "me lady."

From hanging around with him I developed the pattern of using the term "my lady" myself on occasion, delivering it with a British intonation. Over the years I apparently began to overuse it in hallway greetings.

One woman, with whom I interacted briefly three or four times a month, left us unexpectedly and cited among her reasons the fact that I had never taken time to learn her name. Nothing could have been farther from the truth. I had great admiration for her. But because I regularly addressed her as "my lady," not by her name, she concluded that I had no genuine concern for her.

You might consider her reaction as evidence that she was unduly sensitive. But everyone is sensitive, some simply more so than others. And people are particularly sensitive to evidence that they are not valued. That they are not considered worthy of respect.

They therefore take note of small, but significant telltale signs of how much they are valued and respected by leadership. Does their leader make a timely response to their voice mail messages? What about their emails? What about their requests for help or advice?

People presume that we give our time to things that we value most. When we don't have time for them, but seem to have plenty of time for other sundry duties, they lose their confidence in our care for them. It's important, I've learned, to acknowledge receipt of an email or phone message, even when I can't give time immediately to a full response.

Several times a week I send an email which says, "Your message deserves a more thoughtful and thorough response than I can give it right this moment. Here is a quick thought on what you have written about. I will expand on this and provide a more thorough response by such and such a time."

This kind of response is the electronic equivalent of returning a greeting in a hallway. Or paying attention when someone asks us a question. It's a common courtesy which is unfortunately all too uncommon.

To be sure, the Blackberry Age has inundated us with so much email that executives routinely tell me that they are three or four hundred messages behind in making replies. Still, people expect a timely response, even if it is nothing more than heads-up that you may need some time before answering in detail.

Whenever I must postpone a timely and full response to voice messages or emails, I make an effort both to acknowledge that I have received the communiqué, that I will in fact respond to it, and to offer a target deadline by which I will do so.

One of the greatest threats to trust is a pattern of open-ended promises of action to come.

I've discovered that one of the greatest threats to trust is a pattern of open-ended promises of action to come. "I'll get back to you on that" and "I'll give you an answer soon" are not adequate responses from leaders who want to build trust. These types of replies are not specific enough. What does "soon" mean? Two days from now? Three weeks from now? Sometime before the end of the year?

In High-Trust, Peak-Performance Organizations people hold one another accountable. It's difficult to hold someone accountable in a culture of open-ended promises.[50] We are hesitant to approach

---

[50] Arky Ciancutti and Thomas L. Steding refer to this kind of culture as a "random organization," and they estimate that 90% of companies operate as random organizations. By contrast, they offer a model for trust-building built on the principles of commitment and closure, in which nothing is left open-

a person – whether boss, employee, or peer – and say, "You promised an answer soon. Is it soon yet?" It's far easier to say, "You indicated you would have an answer by the end of business yesterday. How do we stand on that?"

It is likewise easier to hold ourselves accountable when we tie specific deadlines to our promises to respond. When I know I have promised a response by Friday, I tend to put the item higher on my priority list as the week progresses. Or if something unexpected develops and I simply cannot get to it by Friday, I'm reminded that I should send a follow-up message explaining my need to adjust the deadline.

Responsiveness is saying, "I will take responsibility for such-and-such, and here is when I will fulfill my responsibility." Then responsiveness means following through in a way that is not only responsible, but also respectful and reaffirming.

ended. *Built on Trust: Gaining Competitive Advantage in Any Organization* (Contemporary Books: Chicago, 2000).

26

The HI-TRUST Formula: Unblemished Fair Play

Nothing brings a leader's integrity into question more quickly than evidence of favoritism. People want a fair and level playing field. That's why they generally frown on nepotism. It also accounts for much of the social backlash against anything that resembles racial or sexual quotas in hiring and promotions.

To have a fair and level playing field, the rules – both written and unwritten – must apply uniformly to everyone. Rules that won't fit everybody are unfit for anybody.

This doesn't mean that leaders are expected to like every worker the same. Or to hold them all in equal esteem. But people do expect leaders to treat everyone fairly, justly, and equitably. Whenever a leader is perceived as less than even-handed in dealing with people, his or her reputation for integrity is in jeopardy and trust is bruised.

Shortly after I took over the reins of the college, classes resumed on campus. Two weeks later one of our seniors discovered that an end-of-summer romantic fling had resulted in pregnancy. This was

173

the early 1980s, when social mores regarding unwed mothers were far more rigid than today.

A few days after we learned of her pregnancy, the dean of students came to my office. He had a form for me to sign, authorizing a refund of her tuition. "What's this?" I asked.

"We have a policy that unmarried girls who become pregnant should return home," he answered.

"How long have we had this rule?" I inquired, having never heard of the policy until this very moment.

"Since long before I came here," he replied.

"During your time on campus how many of our boys have been responsible for some girl becoming pregnant?"

"I'm not sure of the number," he admitted, "but it has happened several times."

"And how many of these young men were sent home?"

"None, that I recall," he said.

"Then the policy just ended," I responded, returning the paperwork to him unsigned. "Tell her she can stay. We can't build trust if we tolerate double standards."

Interestingly, as the dean left my office, he turned, looked back at me, and with a tone of genuine gratitude in his voice said, "Thank you. I've *never* cared for that policy."

Word of the decision spread quickly across the campus. Not everyone agreed with it, including some who accosted me personally on the subject. The decision also cost me a handful of older, more traditionally-minded donors.

But on balance it sent a strong signal to the entire campus community that the new president would treat everyone fairly and with integrity. It proved to be a vital early step in creating the kind of credibility I needed to be a trusted leader.

Treating people uniformly is not about some kind of "corporate communism" in which everyone is given precisely the same privileges, benefits, and rewards. It does mean, however, that at every tier of the organization, people have similar privileges, benefits, and rewards as their peers.

I say "similar privileges, benefits, and rewards" because in some instances it's not practical or even legally possible to have precisely the same work rules for every employee. In highly unionized industries, for example, companies that have made multiple acquisitions or mergers may end up with different union contracts, each with its own set of rules, governing people who work side by side. One of my clients, with this very history, has over 80 different labor contracts inherited from companies they have acquired.

Even in these exceptional circumstances, however, where all of these different rules must coexist, a leader can establish a reputation for being fair, just, and equitable within the limitation of the contractual differences imposed by union agreements.

Whether unionized or not, most companies have standardized employee practices to minimize litigation and to comply with federal and state labor regulations. On the surface, it would seem, all workers are treated uniformly.

For trust to be strong, however, uniform and fair treatment must extend beyond parity in pay and benefits. Uniform treatment of people applies equally to questions like this:

- Is the same performance expectation applied to everyone? Is every person held to the same standard of accountability? Or do some people get by with "slacking off"? Do some workers have more latitude to under-perform than others?

- Is there an "old boys club" (or increasingly, an "old girls club") in the picture? If so, how does it figure into opportunities for advancement or for sought-after assignments?

- Are some workers routinely "kept in the know" more often than their peers?

- Does everyone have an equal opportunity to gain the ear of the boss?

- When kudos are handed out, are some people more prone to receive them than others, based on factors other than performance?

- Do those who "go along" get treated more preferentially than people who probe and question decisions or priorities?

- In bending over backwards to avoid actions that might appear racist or sexist, do leaders end up treating non-minorities in a way that stirs resentment?

Companies that value their record of integrity know that these questions are hardly peripheral. Therefore, these companies go out of their way to hire managers, or potential managers, whose treatment of people is clearly even-handed.

Some companies routinely interview prospective managers in restaurant settings, in part to monitor how courteously the candidate treats waiters, waitresses, and bus boys. These companies assume that candidates who treat service workers courteously and with respect will act the same way toward employees in the company.

This is another wrinkle on an interview technique popularized by the Trammell Crow Company a quarter-century ago. Recruiting from the nation's top MBA programs, the company brought prospective hires to their Dallas corporate headquarters for extensive rounds of interviews. In the course of their visit the candidates inevitably encountered a number of administrative and executive assistants.

Candidates were unaware that these assistants were part of the interview process. Clerical workers were providing feedback to the interviewers on how the prospect treated administrative staffers.

More than one stellar MBA grad failed this part of the interview process and never had an opportunity to work for Trammell Crow.

This interview technique, of course, was hardly a guarantee that newcomers to the company would indeed treat people appropriately. But it at least weeded out those who were least likely to exemplify the company's ideal to treat every individual fairly and with respect.

What it means to be treated fairly, of course, is a matter of personal interpretation. It's not unusual for two people in identical situations, both handled exactly the same way, to voice diverse opinions about whether their treatment was fair.

For this reason, no matter how even-handed a leader tries to be, a charge of being unfair always remains a possibility. Aware of this threat, leaders who want to build trust continually "step outside of themselves" and view their actions from the perspective of other people.

- Is there anything in the leader's action that could be interpreted as a sign of favoritism, cronyism, or prejudice?

- Are decisions made, announced, and discussed in ways that minimize any appearance that people are being treated arbitrarily?

- To a neutral observer, would it look like everyone's views and opinions have an equal opportunity to be heard and considered?

When I go through this type of exercise personally, I put myself in the position of several different people in the organization, people with differing personalities and ways of looking at things. I try to imagine what is going through their minds individually as they look at actions I'm taking and the style of my leadership.

By stepping into a variety of vantage points, viewing myself through a series of individual perspectives, I readily become aware of important nuances that might well go unnoticed were I simply to ask the more generic question, "How will people look at this?"

Personally I've always put a high value on being known for treating people fairly. Thus, one of the most difficult leadership moments for me is to come under attack for being unfair or for violating principles of integrity.

And these moments are particularly stressful when I cannot defend myself without divulging confidential information that shaped my action. To this day I have been unable to recapture the support of people who once backed me strongly, but who now believe I betrayed my values or evidenced weak leadership at a critical moment. In reality I was acting on confidential information which would have given them an altogether different perspective, had they known what I knew.

It's moments like this, in my judgment, that are a true test of a leader's mettle and character. There is a strong temptation to strike back at those who, without all the facts, accuse you unjustly. If, in the face of these circumstances, you can continue to treat your detractors respectfully, fairly, and even-handedly, you will have mastered the resolve to be balanced and equitable in the way you deal with people.

27

The HI-TRUST Formula:
Support and Empowerment

One of the fundamental principles of Trust-Centered Leadership™ is that trust engenders trust. Leaders are more likely to be trusted when they themselves demonstrate trust in their people. And the primary way in which leaders demonstrate trust in their people is through support and empowerment.

Support is one of two elements in the HI-TRUST formula that speaks to the need to feel valued in the SIRVU formula. (The other element is team care, our next topic.)

People tend to believe that leaders who genuinely care for them will provide the support they need to be effective and succeed. Thus, when people feel unsupported by their leader, they also question how much their leader truly values them. And since we are not prone to trust people who do not value us, a non-supportive leader does not typically enjoy high trust.

Support takes a variety of forms, but it basically comes down to three things: encouragement, backing, and resources. Encouragement works hand-in-glove with inspiration, the quality of leadership that most frequently brings out the best in people. It's difficult to envision a discouraged person who simultaneously feels inspired.

Thus, at a personal level, leadership that inspires must begin by creating a supportive, encouraging atmosphere for every member of

the organization. Otherwise, efforts to inspire will have little positive impact on the organization's emotional energy field.

————————————

Early in my career I was associated with Dr. Norvel Young, a
noted leader and visionary who was the chancellor of Pepperdine
University in Malibu, California. When I became an assistant to the
university's president, a long-standing casual acquaintance with
Norvel turned into a daily working relationship.

After a few months on campus, I began to notice that something
inevitably happened when I talked with Norvel. No matter what the
topic of our conversation, I always left our talk feeling upbeat and
positive about myself. Other people, I discovered, had the same experience with him. He was the consummate encourager. But his
encouragement went far beyond occasional encounters on campus.

Periodically the inter-office mail brought a personal note from
him. It was always hand-written, with an expression of thanks and
a word of encouragement for something I had done.

He never cast his comments in broad generalizations, such as
the all-too-common "You're doing a great job!" Instead, he always
cited something specific that I had written, said, or done. I wondered at times how he knew about many of the specifics he mentioned, because I had undertaken them quietly. He was obviously
maintaining a constant vigil for things to commend.

But then I began to pick up another pattern in his encouraging
remarks. He would regularly add to his commendation a statement
along these lines: "This is precisely the kind of attitude and leadership that we must have if we are to achieve our vision to become
noted for . . . ," followed by some phrase from our long-range vision.

He not only encouraged. He also highlighted how your own effort served the larger purposes of the enterprise. He helped you feel
that your contribution was vital to the dream of the university. He
thus built inspiration and developed a clearer commitment to vision
at one and the same time. I soon came to understand why he was so
widely admired and respected.

His lofty standard of encouragement is one that few of us are likely to attain. In truth, I've known only one or two others whose gift for encouragement rivaled his. Nevertheless, his exemplary leadership demonstrates principles that every leader wisely imitates – especially if the goal is to impart encouragement and inspiration by helping people feel personally supported.

But encouragement alone is not enough. To feel supported by leadership, people must also know that their leaders will back them, fight for them, and stand shoulder to shoulder with them when the going gets rough. It's rare to find someone who has not needed a leader to go to bat for him or her at a critical moment.

To feel supported by leadership, people must know that their leaders will back them, fight for them, and stand shoulder to shoulder with them when the going gets rough.

For me that moment came when I was a lieutenant in the naval reserve. Even though I was still a junior officer, my long enlisted service meant that eligibility for retirement was only months away. Then a routine review of my records surfaced a technicality which threatened an immediate end to my career.

The entire issue turned on a vague provision in naval regulations. Few people even knew about the provision, least of all me. And its wording invited a host of conflicting interpretations. But the review panel concluded that I was in violation of the regulation. Thus, vague or not, the technicality was about to put me on the street with no hope of retirement.

At this point a newly-promoted rear admiral came to my rescue. He went to Washington and personally intervened on my behalf. He pleaded my case with three Navy department heads, all of them very senior to him. Without their concurrence, there was no way to salvage my career.

When he returned, he called me into his office. "Don't worry," he said, "you will get enough years to retire. Don't expect anyone to put this promise in writing, because no one from here to the White House wants to make this a test case. But everything has been quietly arranged."

I never asked him to make such an extraordinary effort. He took it upon himself to champion my cause. And I should mention that he took this action shortly after being charged with standing up a new nationwide command which had high-level opposition. Its very survival – and with it his reputation and career – was still hanging in the balance. He needed the support of every possible friend in Washington.

But he willingly cashed in some of his credibility chips for me, when he could have easily treated my circumstances as nothing more than an unfortunate case of a junior officer caught in a bureaucratic bungle. Eighteen years and three promotions later I retired as a captain – but only because I once had a leader who supported me, even at notable risk to himself.

For people to feel that leadership supports them, they must also believe that they have been given proper resources and opportunities to succeed.

Matrix organizations are particularly notorious for violating this principle. The very design of these organizations means that tasking, policies, and procedures converge on most managers from at least two different directions. As a rule, operational directives come from one authority, resources from another.

Unfortunately, the collaboration and coordination between the operational authority and the resource authority are often inadequate, to say the least. I've seen many matrix organizations in which expectations and available resources are sorely unaligned. It takes little imagination to see how a situation like this invites frustration for workers in the ranks.

The solution is not to abandon the matrix philosophy. Matrix organizations are sometimes the best structure to achieve a given strategic vision. But a matrix organization has its drawbacks, including the very problem we have just described. Thus, leaders in matrix organizations must be especially adroit at fighting for the resources that their people need.

However, the struggle for adequate resources is hardly unique to matrix organizations. It's a challenge in any organization. Operational output, after all, drives revenues. Allocating resources drives costs. Consequently, upper management is more prone to approve new operational requirements than to fund additional resources.

For leaders, therefore, it's always tempting to let self-interest trump the energy required to fight doggedly for resources. After all, management promotions, bonuses, and perks are more likely to come from meeting operational goals than from assuring that your people have adequate support. Given this reality, it's all too easy to focus extensively on operational objectives and adopt an attitude of "make-do-as-best-we-can" toward the resource side of the equation.

Trust-Centered Leadership™ always fights for its people in terms of resources. It recognizes that operational objectives are more consistently exceeded with quality in an atmosphere of high trust. And critical to high trust is a consistent pattern of providing proper support and resources for every player on the team.

The issue of support figures prominently in another pivotal arena for trust-building, namely, personal empowerment. Leaders tend to engender trust when they genuinely empower their people. The key phrase in this sentence is "genuinely empower." Not everything that goes by the name "empowerment" deserves the title.

For example, when I asked one upper manager what he meant when he said he empowered people, he responded, "I grant them independent decision-making authority."

"Good," I responded. "And what else do you do?" He paused at length, a puzzled look on his face, then stammered two or three times in an effort to form an articulate reply. He never came up with a substantive response.

For him empowerment merely meant giving people extensive latitude in making decisions. He saw empowerment and delegation as little more than saying, "This is yours. Take it and run with it." He had never made it a priority to assure that adequate tools and resources went hand-in-glove with his delegation of authority and responsibility.

Anyone who has been given decision-making authority, but inadequate tools and resources, is not genuinely empowered. Neither is a person who is otherwise empowered, but who lacks critical skills or know-how. My good friend and fellow-consultant PenDell Pittman describes these types of situations not as delegation, but as dumping.

Leaders tend to engender trust when they genuinely empower their people.

Feeling "dumped on" is all too common in organizational life. In talking to mid-level managers, the one complaint I hear most often is, "They've given me all this additional responsibility, but they expect me to do it with no more people and basically the same budget." (It's the corporate equivalent of the unfunded mandates which Congress routinely passes to the states.)

Somewhere between non-empowerment and full empowerment is a range that we might call "semi-empowerment." This is familiar turf for many managers. They have been given just enough personnel and resources to accomplish their assignment, but only if nothing goes wrong. No delays because a vendor is late on delivery. No change in specifications from the customer. No need for any rework because of engineering mistakes. No labor or cashflow disruptions. If everything goes absolutely without a hitch, the job can be done on time and within budget.

When I deal with situations like this, I usually find that upper management views itself as having done a good job of empowerment. It delegated authority and provided staffing and resources to accomplish the mission.

The "empowered" manager, however, feels stretched so thin in terms of timelines and resources that every decision is immersed in worry and anxiety. The "empowered manager" may also feel stretched thin because an assignment is on the fringe of his or her expertise, or even outside of it altogether.

A major defense firm hired me to coach one of its mid-level managers in charge of a project that was getting further and further behind schedule. The primary culprit was an ever-changing slate of specifications from the Pentagon. The goal was for me help him get more speed and responsiveness out of his organization.

He opened our very first meeting, however, with the announcement that in addition to his primary role, he had been tasked as the acting manager over a functional area that had just lost its director. It was to be a temporary assignment – probably lasting no more than six months – but in an area of engineering with which he had no direct experience.

It soon became apparent that he could not focus fully on his primary duties because he was so distracted by the overwhelming demands of the additional responsibilities. To shoulder this added load he was given no additional administrative assistance. No "crash courses" on the subject matter in his new area of responsibility. No adjustments in deadlines.

Somewhere, I'm sure, someone in upper management was saying, "We've delegated that responsibility to Fred for six months." But they hadn't delegated. They had "dumped" it on him.

Fred needed coaching, which, along with delegated authority and adequate resources, is the third leg of effective empowerment. I call these three the ARC formula for proper empowerment:

- Authority
- Resources

- Coaching

Of the three elements in the ARC formula, coaching is the one most easily overlooked. And I'm using the word "coaching" here in its broadest and most general sense, well beyond the way that we typically delimit executive or business coaching. Coaching, in the sense that I use it here, means providing whatever training, education, or skill enhancement a person may need in order to succeed.

Often empowerment requires no coaching whatsoever. We regularly empower leaders or team members who are already fully equipped for the role we give them. Because this is so commonly the case, it's natural to think of empowerment as solely a matter of delegating authority and providing proper resources.

But often as not, newly empowered people question whether they are fully prepared or competent in one or more arenas of their new assignment. As leaders we may not notice their doubts, for people are astute at projecting more self-confidence than they truly feel.

Moreover, in our performance-driven corporate culture, when aspiring managers and workers receive assignments with career-enhancing potential, they are reluctant to say, "I could really use some coaching on how best to proceed in this new role." It's only later, after the person begins to flounder, that it becomes obvious that coaching would have been helpful.

As a result, delegation and empowerment should always be accompanied by the leader asking, "Is there something we can provide to help you fulfill this assignment?" This question is broad enough to allow the other people to answer in terms of any or all elements of the ARC formula. They may ask for a clarification of their authority. Or they may inquire about needed resources. Or they may note personal reservations about their confidence and competency.

Whatever their response, none of their comments should be treated lightly. But again, I have found that leaders are more likely to pay close attention to responses about authority and resources than to expressions of concern about confidence and competency.

Yet, people who do not feel confident and competent usually envision themselves as needing far more by way of authority and resources than is true when their confidence and sense of personal competence are high. It's incumbent on effective leaders, therefore, to identify where coaching may be needed and to provide it appropriately.

Moreover, once people dig into the details of a task, they often uncover complications, challenges, or personal insecurities they did not anticipate at the outset. Because they failed to foresee these problems at first, they may be hesitant, now that the engagement is underway, to say, "I need some help here."

Yet, deep inside they often long for the leader to ask once more, ""Is there something we can provide to help you fulfill this assignment?" As leaders we need to ask people this question frequently, not merely at the moment of empowerment.

Empowerment, poorly done, actually diminishes trust rather than serving to enhance it. When empowerment does not fully follow the ARC formula, the person "empowered" is left feeling unsupported, but ultimately accountable. Anxiety and worry sets in, most notably worry about being blamed for failure. It's only a small step from this kind of worry to fear. And fear, as it always does, undermines trust.

28

The HI-TRUST Formula: Team Care

One of our deepest drives is to affiliate with others. We yearn to experience a sense of bonding and "belonging," along with pride in the groups to which we belong.

In terms of this sense of belonging, few groups are more important to us than our circle of fellow-workers. Here, as in all high-value groups, we want to "feel like a team" or "feel like a family." It's one reason that the word "team" is now so common as the name for management or business units.

When asked what it means to "feel like a team," people offer a host of descriptions. But their answers always connote a high degree of cohesiveness.

Where high-value groups are not cohesive – or worse, where they are truly dysfunctional – the drive to affiliate and belong goes unfulfilled. People resent it. And in the workplace they typically blame this breakdown on leadership.

That's because we generally look to leaders to help our team "feel like a team." Or failing that, we at least expect our leader to keep undue friction and self-serving agendas from pulling the team apart.

When leaders fail in this regard, there is usually a stiff price to pay. The price tag is damaged credibility as a leader.

For this reason, team care is indispensable to Trust-Centered Leadership™. The object of team care is to root out anything that works to destroy cohesiveness, synergy, and a sense of well-being within the team.

Cohesiveness alone is no assurance that a group truly trusts its leader. But where cohesiveness is weak, trust in the leader is invariably diminished. I've never found an exception to this rule.

This lowered trust stems from one of three causes. In some cases the leader's own conduct has ripped team cohesion apart. The team, in turn, reciprocates by withdrawing trust.

The object of team care is to root out anything that works to destroy cohesiveness, synergy, and a sense of well-being within the team.

In other cases leaders fail to be timely in addressing problems that are working to exact a toll on cohesion. Here it's not so much the leader's action, but his or her inaction that undermines trust.

Then there's the situation in which leaders take over teams where cohesion is already weak. In this instance the leader has contributed nothing, either directly or indirectly, to the loss of cohesion.

Yet, at an unconscious level the group is watching to see if the new leader can build a cohesive team. If not, the group concludes that their leader is inadequate for the job. And again they withhold their trust.

One way or another, then, workers hold the leader accountable for weak team cohesion. And it's proper for them to do so. The absence of team cohesion is always symptomatic of one or more of the following:

- the absence of a compelling, unifying goal which pulls everyone together

- poor or inadequate communication to keep everyone "on the same page"

- widespread distrust within the team

- self-serving agendas which have been elevated above team objectives

All four of these conditions reflect adversely on the quality of leadership.

- Clearly the duty of articulating a compelling, unifying goal falls squarely on the shoulders of the leader.

- So, too, does the responsibility for maintaining appropriate levels of communication within the organization.

- Equally, leaders who do not uproot causes of distrust within the team are ignoring a fundamental obligation.

- And finally, leaders must always be held accountable if they allow team members to get away with self-serving agendas that impair team effectiveness.

Some teams manage to be cohesive in spite of weak leadership. This is most often found in organizations where turnover is minimal and team members build long-term friendships and camaraderie among themselves. When interpersonal relationships are deep and resilient, organizations can maintain a tight-knit atmosphere, even when leadership falls short.

During my Navy career I saw this very thing in a number of naval reserve squadrons. Unlike active duty components of the armed forces, reserve units tend to maintain a somewhat stable personnel roster for years on end. Relatively few people transfer in and out of the organization. Members of the unit work and train together for years at a time, which leads to lasting, life-long relationships.

But the unit commander is usually a newcomer to the group. The Navy usually assigns commanding officers to units in which they have not previously served. Should a new commander prove to be a weak leader, the unit does not fall apart.

Instead, the unit tends to adopt an attitude of "we'll just wait this one out." The rank and file knows that within two years the current skipper will be gone. They simply wait patiently for the replacement.

Meanwhile, the quality of the long-standing relationships within the unit holds the team together. Morale and effectiveness may suffer. They usually do. But overall cohesiveness remains intact.

Such organizations are a rare breed. With today's rapid turnover among employees, few teams have large numbers of deep interpersonal relationships. Thus, in the face of weak leadership, team cohesiveness becomes elusive, to say the least.

Moreover, when cohesiveness breaks down, the breakdown becomes common knowledge all too quickly. The rumor mill goes to work. Disgruntled team members talk to friends who tell others who tell others.

Upper management soon is aware of the problem and is not likely to wait long to take action. From what I've observed as a business coach and consultant, the inability for managers to overcome team strife or discontent is one of the most common causes for early termination or reassignment.

This is because higher management loses trust in managers who cannot maintain team cohesiveness. And among members of the team, trust in the leader erodes even faster. When people say, "We're not really a team around here," they are questioning the competence of their leader, even if they don't say so explicitly.

An entire industry has been built around team-building, from communications workshops to challenge-outings and ropes courses.

All of these can be helpful tools. But the front line responsibility for building team cohesiveness lies with the leader.

I've noticed that leaders who fail to build cohesiveness generally fall into three identifiable categories. First, there is the leader who has an inordinate need to be liked. As a rule, this type of leader postpones confrontation as long as possible. The drive to be liked stands in the way of timely, decisive discipline when people are being disruptive or sowing discord within the team.

Disruptive forces in a team don't tend to disappear just because we ignore them – no more than a painful rock in your shoe goes away just because you keep walking.

Not that such leaders never confront. Many times they do. But only after so much time has passed – and so much damage has occurred – that telling damage has been done both to the cohesiveness of their team and to their own credibility as a leader.

Disruptive forces in a team don't tend to disappear just because we ignore them – no more than a painful rock in your shoe goes away just because you keep walking. I've never talked to a leader who, in the long-run, regretted having taken immediate, decisive action when someone was disrupting team cohesiveness. But I've talked to scores of leaders who must contend with the lasting impact of waiting too long to confront.

A second group of leaders allow cohesiveness to erode because the offending party is "too valuable to lose." Rather than run the risk of losing a star, they make a calculated gamble. They take the chance that team cohesiveness can successfully sustain any injury from the star's problem behavior.

Successful leaders, like successful athletic coaches, never make this often fatal mistake. They never compromise on team unity, even if it costs them a star player.

Recently I facilitated a day-long meeting with a client who was only weeks into his new role as a regional manager. His entire management team was part of the meeting.

Later, as we were parting, he said to me, "The fellow who was across the table from you today won't be with us next week. In terms of revenue, he is one of our best performers. But he constantly undercuts team cooperation, and he seems unwilling to change. This team will never attain its peak potential so long as he creates disarray."

This manager's statement bespeaks a rare kind of courage. How was he going to justify to his own superiors a decision to oust a top performer? And what about the reaction of his team? How would they receive the loss of a top-performing colleague? His absence would surely mean a drop in the team's total financial performance – at least for the first few months. How would team members respond when they were pressed to meet financial targets without one of their strongest contributors?

Yet, in the long run, his was a wise decision. The question is not so much what will happen to overall financial performance in the next 90 days, but how much stronger overall performance will be in a year due to greater trust and cohesiveness within the team.

A third type of leader who looks the other way while team cohesiveness suffers is the one who does not fully sense the power of synergy. Sadly, there are still people in leadership positions who view their team as simply a group of individual contributors. They don't recognize that highly energized, collaborative teams quickly become more than the sum of their parts.

This "blind spot" is particularly common in companies and organizations where people promote into management from career paths as "sole performers."

It happens regularly in engineering, where subject matter experts who rarely left their cubicle are put in charge of a team. It happens in finance, where people who distinguished themselves as solo auditors or analysts are promoted to management. It happens in sales, in brokerage firms, and in service industries where technicians work independently in the field before rising to management posts.

When teams transcend the sum of their parts, they are inevitably teams with high levels of trust.

In career paths like these, people come into management having perhaps never experienced a truly synergistic team. Once they move into management, they may believe that they have created team cohesiveness when in fact they only have a team whose members periodically confer with one another. Willingness to confer, in and of itself, is a far cry from the kind of creative synergy that makes a team more than the sum of its parts.

And when teams do transcend the sum of their parts, they are inevitably teams with high levels of trust. People can confer and compare notes without truly trusting one another. But they can't form a synergistic, peak-performance team without trust.

Since cohesiveness, synergy, and team trust are so inseparable, Trust-Centered Leadership™ puts no less emphasis on team care than it does on character, integrity, and performance. If our goal is to build a High Trust, Peak Performance organization, it is never an option to pursue other elements of the SIRVU and HI-TRUST formulas, while ignoring team care.

Why? Because other elements of the SIRVU and HI-TRUST formulas serve to increase trust in the leader. But they do not assure greater cohesiveness within the team. People may have a reasonable level of trust in their leader, yet still feel like they are part of a disjointed group rather than a true team.

This feeling of disjointedness, in turn, limits the amount of trust people place in their leader. As we said at the top of the chapter, people hold leadership accountable when teams are not cohesive.

And if the problem is not remedied readily, the level of trust in the leader inevitably suffers.

That's why Trust-Centered Leadership™ pursues team care purposefully. Sustained peak performance is possible only when leaders are fully trusted and their team is deeply cohesive.

Trust Is Power

How do you end a book about building trust? The topic is inexhaustible. That's largely because trust is at the heart of every healthy human relationship. And because the variety of relationships is endless, the nuances of trust-building are equally endless.

Let me conclude, therefore, by emphasizing the one overarching idea that I want you to carry away. It's the idea embodied in the phrase "trust is power." People entrust power to those whom they trust. Conversely, the person who is trusted has the power of influence without resorting to the power of coercion.

In a word, only love rivals trust in its power to influence. Moreover, in the arena of leadership, trust is often more powerful than love. For even love resists the leadership of someone it distrusts.

Trust grants power while also minimizing the need to resort to power.

So let me conclude by taking you back to the moment when I first discovered the transcendent power of trust. It happened almost five decades ago, one Sunday afternoon in the middle of a muddy river in East Texas.

As background, let me preface the story by telling you a little about my father. A noted sports columnist once described him as a "leathery outdoorsman," and a more fitting phrase could not have been found. He was the consummate outdoorsman, as astute at survival in the water and the wild as anyone I've ever known.

And leathery? He was every bit as tough as leather. As a young man he earned his way by contracting to kill alligators out of lakes and rivers – and occasionally wrestling one in a side show to make a few extra bucks. And thirty years later, as I was growing up in his household, much of our livelihood still depended on hunting, trapping, and commercial fishing.

Which is what brought us that Sunday afternoon to the banks of the Sabine River. At the time there were no flood control lakes on the Sabine. And after several days of heavy rains, the river was rising rapidly.

We knew that with the higher water, big catfish – 30, 40, 60-pounders, some even larger – would soon start moving upstream. Our goal was to have our nets in the water before they made their run.

So shortly after noon Dad and I stuffed 200 feet of trammel nets into burlap sacks, tossed them into the back of a battered Ford pickup, and rattled off to the river. Then we backpacked the nets to a remote stretch of water where the river banks were steep and the current ran swift and deep.

There we shed our clothes, slipped into the water, and hauled the first net in behind us. We soon had it stretched to the other side – only to discover something altogether unexpected.

The current had carved a gaping hollow underneath the river bank, and the opening was now so big that even the largest fish could evade our nets. Something had to be done to plug that hole.

Looking around for a solution, Dad looked across the river and spied our clothes. Near them, slightly farther downstream, was the large burlap sack which moments before had held the net.

"Get me that sack," he said. "We can fill it with mud and stuff it in this opening."

So I dutifully struck out to the other side, retrieved the sack, and started back across, towing the sack behind me – a fateful and almost fatal miscalculation.

Can you imagine how heavy a burlap sack becomes when it's soaking wet? And here I was, using one arm to fight upstream against the current, all the while towing the dead weight of that sack in my other hand.

Suddenly, without warning, in the middle of the river – at the very deepest point – every muscle in my body gave out. There was not another stroke in my being. Thrashing frantically to stay afloat, I was already swallowing water, all the while clinging to that burlap sack like the proverbial drowning man grasping at straws.

Just then Dad barked out a sharp command: "Drop the sack! Get a breath and go under!"

"Oh, yes," I thought. "I need to turn loose of the sack. And I need to . . . WHAT?? Get a breath and GO UNDER??" The *last* thing a drowning man wants to do is to put his head beneath the water!!

Yet, amazingly, because I trusted Dad's instincts in the water so deeply, I complied without hesitation. I released the sack, threw back my head, gulped down a breath of air, and tucked my head below the water.

The next few moments seemed like an eternity. Just when I could hold out no longer, when every muscle in my chest was burning from squeezing the last molecule of oxygen from my lungs, I felt his huge, powerful hands slip under me and lift me to the surface. It was all over as quickly as it had begun.

But how had he found me in that muddy, murky water where visibility was only a foot or so at best?

Well, there was genuine wisdom in his rather strange command. He knew that as long as I clutched that heavy sack, it would only pull me down and out of sight. But freed of its weight and with my lungs filled with air from a deep breath, I would sink no more than a few inches beneath the surface. That, then, allowed him to keep an eye on me as he sped to my rescue.

And so it was, in that moment of life and death, that I learned a lesson which 20 years later helped me save a college and which has guided me as a leader wherever I've served. It's a lesson about the power of trust. When people genuinely trust their leader, the unthinkable becomes possible.

A drowning teenager will choke back his panic and drop his head beneath the water. A faculty, already weeks behind on salary, will commit to stay on. Donors, still not sure of the future, will dig into their pockets once more. Trust is power.

Develop yourself as a trusted leader, and people will knock down the door to follow you.

And in the post-Enron world, trust is more powerful than ever. With our spiraling trust deficit, people are eager for trusted leadership to emerge, whether in business, politics, or institutional life. They long for leaders who use the SIRVU and HI-TRUST formulas as guides.

You can be the leader they seek. Master the SIRVU and HI-TRUST formulas through constant practice. Hone your trust-building skills every day.

An old proverb says, "Build a better mousetrap, and the world will beat a path to your door." I would add a corollary. Develop yourself as a trusted leader, and people will knock the door down to follow you.